VAGUS NERVE EXERCISES

Daily Exercises and Stimulation Techniques

To Activate Your Natural Healing Power

And Cure Inflammation, Anxiety, Stress,

Chronic Illness and More Diseases

TABLE OF CONTENTS

INTRODUCTION

Your body contains over 60 trillion cells (Habib, 2019). Electrical signals are continuously firing back and forth from the brain to all the organs of your body, and the highways along which those signals are carried are your nerves.

The nervous system is possibly the body's most complex system. In many ways, it is the system we know the least about. Scientists have attempted to break this system down into smaller categories to make it easier to understand, easier to study, and easier to work with. However, as with most things, the more we learn about the nervous system, the more questions we have. As we continue to study the body, it's often the case that many of the things we once believed were true turn out to be false.

For example, we once believed that the basic function of the nervous system was to send signals back and forth from the brain to the body's various organs. While we still know this to be true, we are also discovering that that job is far more important than we initially realized. Nerves themselves play a far more active role than was once supposed, and the vagus nerve is one of the most important channels of information in the entire body.

What is commonly referred to as the "vagus nerve" is actually a vast network of nerves, all branching out from one core trunk located in the spinal cord. While the existence of vagus nerves is undisputed, some scientists believe that the entire vagus system is one continuous unit, while others believe that the "vagus system" is actually a series of interconnected nerves that should be considered a fourth branch of the autonomic nervous system. The idea that there is just one single, uninterrupted vagus nerve with a multitude of branches is often referred to as "polyvagal theory." Polyvagal theory ascribes to the idea that the vagus nerve is built up of two parallel structures, one on either side of the body, that each connect to a core trunk located in the spinal cord. If this theory is indeed correct (which an increasing number of studies seem to indicate), this would make the vagus nerve the only nerve that originates in the brainstem and has branches throughout the entire body.

There are branches of the vagus nerve responsible for regulating cellular processes in the heart, lungs, throat and esophageal muscles, liver, stomach, pancreas, gallbladder, spleen, kidneys, small intestine, and the large intestine. In fact, the vagus nerve is the main connection between the gut's microbiome and the brain. The culture of bacteria in your gut that helps your body to break down and absorb food is in direct contact with the vagus nerve, and is the channel through which most of its signals are sent up to the brain.

Remember that there are three branches of the autonomic nervous system: the enteric system that regulates the gastrointestinal tract, *the sympathetic nervous system* that *regulates our "fight-or-flight" state*, and *the parasympathetic nervous system* that *regulates our "rest-*

and-digest" state. The vagus nerve has branches in all three of these systems, which means that this single nerve, by itself, makes up most of the autonomic nervous system. In fact, almost all of the nerves in the parasympathetic and enteric branches are vagus nerves.

This guide has been designed to delve deeper into this fascinating subject and enable the reader to gain a greater understanding of the function of the vagus nerve and the possibilities of stimulating it to have real benefits on the organs of our body by promoting a good general psycho-physical state.

CHAPTER 1. WHAT IS VAGUS NERVE

First, we are going to start with a little bit of science, then some explanation for people who are not research scientists or brain surgeons. We will be delving into some examples, both imaginary and personal stories that happened to real people. But first, we need to explore exactly what the vagus nerve is and how it interacts with the rest of the body in order to fully comprehend its impact on so many different areas of our lives.

The vagus nerve is the longest cranial nerve in the body, reaching out from the brain stem as a pair of nerves, one for controlling each side of the body. It got its name from the Latin word for wanderer (vagus) because it wanders throughout the entire body. This is an apt description as the vagus nerve impacts in some way nearly every organ in the body.

The vagus nerve prevents inflammation, acts as a conduit for information from the visceral lower abdominal organs to the brain, controls breathing, strengthens memory power, controls heart rate, and relays information from the facial muscles to the brain stem. The vagus nerve even has a connection to our taste buds.

Additionally, the vagus nerve impacts our creativity, our higher cognitive functions, and decision making.

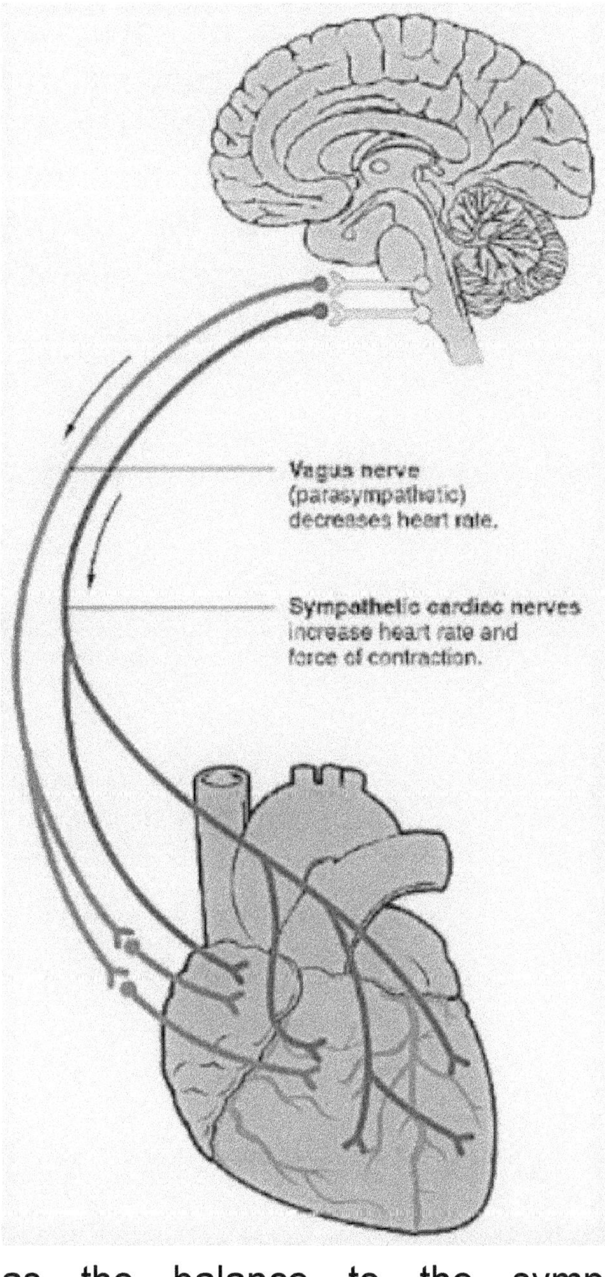

Acting as the balance to the sympathetic

nervous system, it helps to calm you when you are stressed, sending out signals to all the organs to release calming enzymes and proteins, thus providing the balance for the body's autonomic fight, flight, or freeze response, and stress levels.

Form and Function of the Vagus Nerve

The human body has twelve cranial nerves that extend directly from the brain and brain stem, unlike spinal nerves that attach directly to the spinal cord.

These cranial nerves act as information pathways from all the various parts of the body to the brain. The vagus nerve is the longest cranial nerve, leading from the brain, along the jawline and extending down between the internal jugular vein and the internal carotid artery, through the neck and chest, into the abdomen and reaching down to the viscera, or intestines. This nerve mostly works to bring information from the organs to the central nervous system, so most of its information is going from the organs to the brain.

The vagus nerve is actually a bundle of two, the ventral and the dorsal. The ventral vagus extends from the right side to the heart and lungs impacting both heart rate and respirations, and into the facial muscles, eyes, and into the inner ear. You might notice that these are all parts of our body that deal with social engagement. This will be important later on. This part of the vagus nerve is myelinated. Myelin is a fatty substance that surrounds our nerve cell axons. It insulates them and acts as a means of speeding up the process by which those axons carry information. The greater the amount of myelinization present, the faster the speed of the information being carried to and from the brain. The dorsal vagus extends from the left down into the abdomen and the lower organs, the guts. It is this part of the vagus that you are referring to when you say you have "a gut feeling" or someone "gets on your last nerve." This portion of the vagus nerve has no myelin.

All these descriptions give the sense that the vagus nerve is just one long line, but in fact it is a branching system that reaches into every part of your body like a tree root in soil, as the picture shows.

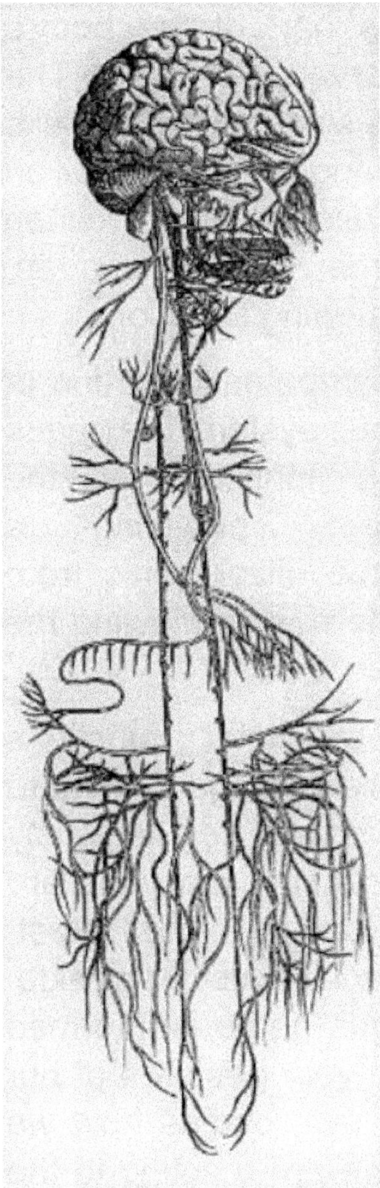

The vagus nerve is part of the body's parasympathetic nervous system. The sympathetic nervous system is what kicks in when you are in danger. It provides you with the fight or flight instinct when presented with some sort of sudden, unexpected, or threatening situation.

As part of the parasympathetic portion of the autonomic nervous system, the vagus nerve acts as an inhibitor for the sympathetic system, providing a counterbalance to the initial panic from the sympathetic system, and allowing the body to calm down.

The vagus nerve's motor functions extend to the medulla oblongata - where autonomic responses are regulated by the brain, while its sensory functions are directly tied to the cranial neural crest, where the body's facial muscles reside. This means the vagus nerve is informed and impacted by the very gestures of our face. We teach our own bodies how we feel based on how we are reacting to the world around us.

The vagus nerve is connected to the neuroception system of the body which helps us gather information to determine the safety of our environment on an unconscious level.

PHYSICAL DAMAGE TO THE VAGUS NERVE

The vagus nerve can be damaged by diabetes, upper respiratory viral infections, alcoholism, or through an accident during an operation. Stress, fatigue, anxiety, and even bad posture can also have a negative impact on the vagus nerve. The symptoms of vagal nerve damage include loss of the gag reflex, difficulty speaking or complete loss of voice, a speaking voice that is hoarse or wheezy, trouble drinking liquids, unusual heart rate, abnormal blood pressure, pain in the ear, decreased production of stomach acid, nausea or vomiting, and abdominal bloating or pain. The health of the vagus nerve can be checked by testing the heart variability rate, the difference in heart rate between exhalation and inhalation. A steady, smooth rate indicates the health of it.

Another aspect of the vagus nerve is that fully 80% of all the information is traveling from the organ systems up this nerve to the brain, while only the remaining 20% of its function involves information traveling down the nerve to the organs and lower systems. We usually think of the brain as being the originator of all information regarding our surroundings, but really it is the individual systems that begin the process, such as the eyes that see telling us what our surroundings look like, ears that hear telling us what sounds are nearby, the nose gathering in and reacting to scents constantly, and the taste buds on the tongue telling us what we need to know about the food we put in our mouth.

Skin receptors tell us what the air feels like, what we are touching at the time, and many other things that we only pick up on a subconscious level. Being aware of this helps us understand the importance of our nervous system and its essential functions.

CHAPTER 2. VAGUS NERVE FUNCTIONS

It allows us to feel sensation in the skin of the ear

The vagus nerve allows us to feel touch, wetness and temperature on the skin of the tragus, auricle and the external auditory canal of the ear. These parts are located in the central sections of the ear and acupuncture is taking advantage by using these locations to stimulate the vagus nerve.

It manages the liver and its functions

The liver alone performs hundreds of functions in the body, with around 500 duties, it is no lightweight. One of these functions, the one I am currently interested in is the regulating of the blood flow throughout the body. The arms are legs are prioritized when the body enters fight or flight mode, therefore blood is diverted to them. This activates the muscles and gives the arms and legs the strength required to take the appropriate action. It also cause a decrease in the flow of blood in the liver but it doesn't matter because the filtration and digestion are not prioritized at that moment. The process is reversed when the body returns to rest mode. Filtration and digestion becomes a priority again and the blood flow to the liver is increased.

The liver also produces bile and bile salt which are transported to the gallbladder and small intestine. The vagus nerve indirectly controls both the production and the transportation of bile and bile salt. Experts have noticed that cholangiocytes, the cells responsible for both actions are active when the vagus nerve is active. The vagus nerve activates the cholangiocytes cells and to produce the bile and bile salt then transport it to the small intestine.

The liver's detoxification of fat-soluble toxins to create water-soluble waste is undertaken in two stages. One of the duties of the bile is to hold the stool, which contains some of the waste products. The rest of these waste products are held in our sweats and urine.

Bile salts on the other hand, move with fat molecules from the digestive system and through the enterocytes cells (lining the small intestine) into the bloodstream. Fat can only be absorbed in the presence of bile salt and they will likely end up in the stool, causing fatty stool. The fat is also important to the body.

It maintains our blood pressure

The vagus nerve transmit information to and fro the kidneys to aid the control of fluids and water flowing into the bloodstream. The kidney filters the fluids and water using the kidney glomeruli, and removes toxins from the body, herby maintaining the blood pressure. The blood vessels send signals to the brain when the body is under stress. The brainstem then transmits signals to the kidney, through the vagus nerves. The signals trigger the kidney to increase the blood pressure. The kidney accomplishes this by constricting its blood vessels to reduce the quantity of water it filters out of the bloodstream.

This process is reversed when the body is starts returning to rest mode. The kidney receives signals to increase the quantity of water it filters out of the blood stream. The vagus nerve and sympathetic nerves are not solely responsible for these actions, as the hormones are also involved.

A dysfunctional vagus nerve can cause over-activation of the stress hormones in the adrenal glands which couples with the immune autonomic system's response to it to result in high blood pressure and hypertension.

It controls our heart rate

The vagus nerve ensures that the heartbeat is at a comfortable rate. The activities of the vagus nerve help the heart generate the right reaction to situations and avoid stress. The beating of the heart allows it to pump blood into body cells and move toxins to organs that will store and dispose them. The vagus nerve connects to the sinoatrial node, a tissue that sends electrical signals to the two thinner chambers of the heart (the atria), and the atrioventricular node, a tissue that controls the pumping rate and contraction pressure of the two larger chambers of the heart (the ventricles). Each connection is separate and direct.

The vagus nerve stimulates the nervous system to make the heart increase the pressure of the contraction of the ventricles, thus increasing the heart rate, when in fight or flight mode. The situation is reverse when the body is returning to rest mode, the heart is activated to reduce the pressure of the contraction of the ventricles and decrease the heart rate.

It activates the Gallbladder to empty its contents

The gallbladder is like a save that holds bile until it is required during digestion of the next meal. The taste buds transmit signals to the brain, when you eat. These signals also contain information about the macronutrients they sensed in every bite of the food. If fat is being consumed, the central nervous system transmits signals to the liver and the gallbladder which prepares to release fat into the small intestine.

The gallbladder then activates the smooth muscle walls that line it, after receiving the alert signal. The muscle walls will pump bile into the small intestine through the bile duct. This signal is transmitted by the vagus nerve and without it the gallbladder wouldn't know when to empty the gall bladder. The gallbladder then becomes and remains full resulting in a medical condition called the obstructive cholestasis. Obstructions due to gallstone are one of the most common medical conditions that affect the gallbladder. The resulting surgery to remove the gallstones is one of the most common surgeries performed annually in the United States. The surgery is called cholecystectomy and it is usually recommended when patients begin to feel pain resulting from obstructions like gallstones. Gallstones are painful and it takes a while for them to form in the gallbladder. This is usually due to long term dysfunction of the vagus nerve. A dysfunctional vagus nerve results in the gallbladder not transporting the bile and bile duct out. They tend start to crystalline and form stones, the longer they remain in the gallbladder.

This condition is one of the earliest effects of a dysfunctional vagus nerve, it also doesn't exactly require surgery to fix although surgery has been the common route. The gallbladder can remove the gallstones, if it starts functioning optimally. Some exercise that will help you activate the gallbladder will be provided in this book.

It controls the motor function of the digestive tract

The digestive tract is a long and intricate pathway consisting of various organs. Food must move from one end of the digestive tract (the mouth) until the waste material (stool, urine and sweat) are removed from the body. All these movements are stimulated by the vagus nerve. When we take a bite of food, we usually chew it until it can be swallowed.

After swallowing the food is transported through the lengths of the digestive tract. The first step is the pharynx, which is located at the back of the throat. The autonomous system take control, as every action from this point is subconscious. The vagus nerve takes control. It triggers the smooth muscles lining the walls of the gut to push the food. Every bite generates a reaction from the muscles which in turn transmits a signal to the brain. The brain replies back with a signal to start motor actions and push the food down the gut. The process is called peristalsis and the vagus nerve is the medium when information is transmitted in both directions. The long journey through the gut allows the body to extract nutrients from the food and separate unwanted constituents. This activity and the length of the gut make the process more complex than it looks.

A dysfunctional vagus nerve results in a disruption of this process. The muscles and nerves are impaired, and it can result in diarrhea and chronic constipation. A simple and common cause of this dysfunction is not chewing the food properly and rushing your food. The rest mode is essential for digestion but most people in the modern world eat their food in the fight of flight mode. The body prioritizes action over digestion in this stance and the digestive process suffers.

It controls the release of digestive enzymes from the Pancreas

---

The pancreas produces and secretes digestive enzymes into the small intestine. The sensory intestinal cells and taste buds of the tongue transmit a signal to the brain. This signal contains information about the macronutrients present in the food. This include how much and how fast fat, carbohydrate and protein where consumed. The information is used to determine the kind of digestive enzyme required and the quantity in which they are needed. These enzymes (for example amylase, lipase and protease) are required to digest the ingested food and they also help to optimize the usage of the basic nutrients generated from the digested food.

If the food contains fat, the pancreas secretes lipase which breaks down the fat into triglycerides and free fatty acid. If the food contains protein, it secretes protease which breaks the protein into amino acids. If the food contains carbohydrate, the pancreas secrets amylase which breakdowns the carbohydrates to simple sugars.

The simple forms can then be absorbed by the body and use to facilitate cell functions. Amino acids are used by the cells to produce protein, receptors, peptide hormones, intracellular signaling molecules and neurotransmitters. Simple sugar and free fatty acids are the main resources for producing energy. Cholesterol is functions as a precursor for steroid hormones like, cortisol, testosterone and estrogen. Every one of these is required for optimal functionality of the human body. A dysfunction in any department can set of a cycle of disaster.

It manages the insulin and blood sugar levels

Some of the most rampant health problems today include obesity and diabetes. These two problems are a result of an unhealthy lifestyle resulting in weight problems and blood sugar level problems, respectively.

When the human body is under stress, the body activates fight or flight mode. This mode is a result of evolution and a deeply ingrained instead developed from the earlier days of man, when most of the creatures on earth were larger than him. Flight was the major option until fight also became more prominent. These two, fight or flight are our response to a threat. When the body is in fight of flight mode, the balance shifts to the sympathetic nervous system and more adrenaline is released, especially cortisol. Cortisol raises the blood sugar level by instigating the creation of glucose from protein and fat available in the liver. The process is called gluconeogenesis.

The nervous system tries to funnel out energy to the essential organs and body parts required to make the next decision and act on it. The legs and ands are the main targets. These creates short term fuel, glucose in a process called gluconeogenesis and releases it into the bloodstream. Blood flow to the legs and arms are increased because they have been prioritized. The muscles of these body parts are strengthened by the increased blood flow, making the fight or flight action easier, faster and more effective.

This system may fall short in its timing by remaining active for longer than required. Due to the stressful environment of the modern world, the body is almost always in a fight or flight mode. Several modern activities from work, transportation, managing our finances and even some mundane daily activities contribute to the stressful environment. This situation leaves the body in constant stress and reduces the amount of time spent in rest and digest mode. The liver keeps producing glucose hereby increasing the blood sugar levels at an unhealthy rate and on a long term.

The body reacts to this by trying to reduce the amount of glucose in the blood. This is accomplished by triggering the pancreas to produce insulin, a chemical that signals the cells of the body to absorb glucose from the blood and convert it to energy. As this is a long-term problem the pancreas keep producing insulin and the insulin keeps signaling the cells of the body to absorb glucose from the blood. Over time the cells become resistant to insulin, and they begin to reject the messages. After other cells have stopped absorbing glucose from the blood, the adipocytes (adipose tissue) is the only one that keeps absorbing the glucose and it receives all the messages from the insulin and absorbs as many glucose as it can.

The adipose tissue is also called the fat tissue and it can be found in every part of the body although it is mostly concentrated in the stomach. This is how people gain weight and it ultimately becomes type II diabetes. At this stage the pancreas has produced so much insulin that it became worn out. People with diabetics are usually prescribed insulin or medications that stimulate insulin sensitivity in the cells. Ultimately, high blood sugar levels can lead to obesity, insulin resistance and diabetes. The high blood sugar levels may be caused by a high sugar diet, chronic overeating and chronic stress.

It manages inflammation in the digestive tract

The vagus nerve transmits information about the responses of the immune system between various organs of the body and the brain. The pathway through which these signals travel is called the cholinergic anti-inflammatory pathway. The cholinergic anti-inflammatory pathway connects the cells of the autoimmune system and one of its most active locations is in the gut. It uses the neurotransmitter Acetylcholine (ACh) to transmit signals that calm the immune system in other to reduce inflammation.

The signals transmitted by the vagus nerves from the spleen and thymus to the brain increase noticeable due to the increasing production of stress chemicals such as lipopolysaccharides (LPS).LPS is a toxin generated and released into the gut by certain bacterial, pathogen and viruses. It is a good thing that the autoimmune system is constantly on alert due to the stress-inducing environment and ready to engage the invaders. The white blood cells send out a signal that is transmitted to the GALT (Gut-Associated Lymphoid tissues). This triggers the sympathetic nerves and a stress response. Adrenaline also called norepinephrine (NE), a neurotransmitter receives a signal from the sympathetic nerves. The white blood cells are then triggered by the adrenaline and they proceed to combat the invading pathogens and stressor chemicals.

This system is a very important and efficient one that requires a well-defined start and stop button or instructions. The vagus nerve performs this function it keeps the autoimmune system and the generated inflammation in check. The vagus nerve accomplishes this by transmitting ACh from the gut to the parts of the body where inflammation is building up. The ACh's job is to counteract the inflammation which is a reaction to adrenalin and the sympathetic nerves.

This makes the system, in simple terms a balance between sympathetic and parasympathetic nerves. Sympathetic nerves trigger a cycle that results in inflammation and parasympathetic nerves try to shut down inflammation after it has done its job.

It controls the autoimmune system

The immune system is the body's self-defense network. It protects us save from infections. It also needs to be managed and the vagus nerve does a good job of doing these. This mostly consists of transmitting the activating signal at the right time and the deactivation signal at the right time. If the immune system is not activated at the right time the infection will keep damaging the body cells, the immune system combats this. The immune system will start attacking healthy cells if it is not instructed to stop after eliminating the infection. The immune system consists of leukocytes (white blood cells), which transmit sensors that inspect the body for the likelihood of toxins and infectious pathogens. The white blood cells wander the bloodstream and denote the nutrients and other materials that enter the bloodstream. They then signal white blood cells to perform their functions and eliminate unwanted constituents and invaders.

White blood cells that discover invaders and infections near their location will assess the threat and relay SOS messages, asking for support by releasing cytokines (a form of protein), in the area. This attracts nearby white blood cells that will provide back up in combating the invading pathogens. The vagus nerve detects the cytokines (SOS messages) and relays the signal to the brain to the brain informing it about the beginning of a potential inflammation.

According to recent research, the vagus nerve can differentiate between the different types of cytokines and therefore it can tell the brain the specific type of inflammation that is building up.

The immune system contains several types of white blood cells. Examples include the mast cells, the macrophages, natural killer cells, neutrophils, monocytes and dendritic cells (phagocytes such as lymphocytes, eosinophils and basophil).

The purpose of this book is to inform you about the functioning of the vagus nerve and its importance, but above all to show you how to activate it effectively.

CHAPTER 3. DISEASES CONNECTED WITH VAGUS NERVE

The vagus nerve sure is the superhighway in the bodies of the living organisms but it often gets bumpy and rough under some circumstances. There are also some diseases that are linked with the X cranial nerve. Bear in mind that the vagus nerve either drives one's wellness or it drives one's disease. The vagus nerve dysfunction is the most common factor that generates many diseases in the human body. The person works fine for a few weeks when the vagus nerve dysfunction surfaces. There are a few perceived causes of damage that occurs to the vagus nerve and that are:

- Diabetes: The diabetes causes the level of blood sugar to rise exponentially.

This ends up damaging the blood vessels that relate to the vagus nerve and eventually, the vagus nerve gets affected hence, gets damaged. This is one reason it fails to get activated and causes a lot of diseases to attack.

- Toxic exposure: There might be some toxic chemicals or bodies that prove to be harmful for the organs present inside the human body. The harm these chemicals or bodies cause are prone to affect the vagus nerve as well which causes the big diseases to easily get access to the human body and do their work.
- Infection: When any infection spreads in the body, it causes all the cranial nerves to be affected therefore, the vagus nerve gets affected too. This halts the vagus nerve from

functioning well hence, it has trouble getting activated.

- Any injury in brain or the atrophy injury: When this happens, the brain and the nerves face nutrients deprivation which stops the proper functioning of the vagus nerve. Keep away from things that could cause you such injuries.
- VNS surgical complications: The vagus nerve stimulation device implant is done to regulate the stimulation of the vagus nerve but at times, when the doctors are not really equipped with experience or they end up making a mistake. The surgery sometimes ends up damaging the vagus nerve profusely which causes it to stop its functions abruptly. Hence, it is necessary for the patients to seek a doctor who knows what he/she is doing.

Because, there is no possible cure for the vagus nerve damage.

Hence, the patient remains oblivious for a little time until finally, the symptoms begin to appear. You will begin to feel sick at first, not the go-to-doctor bad sick but the light sick. Then the cold would kick in and soon after, you'll be unable to get out of the bed; and the energy will drop down very fast.

These are the minor symptoms which tell you that you are experiencing the vagus nerve dysfunction while the major ones are not very pleasing. However, the diseases that are associated with the vagus nerve dysfunction are in a great number which highlights the fact how crucial this nerve is and how important it is to keep it running smooth. Now, let's talk about the diseases that the vagus nerve dysfunction causes:

Diseases caused by Vagus Nerve dysfunction

1) **Brainstem lesion:**

This refers to the damaged tissue within the brain due to either an injury or problems in the immune system which is dealt by vagus nerve. This damage causes the memory loss, neck pain, seizures, vision problems, fever, lack of appetite, nausea and the mood changes. All of these problems are handled by vagus nerve but when the vagus nerve dysfunction occurs, the problems get the best of the poor brain.

2) **Weight management and appetite:**

The vagus nerve deals with the intake of food and when it is excessive, the vagus nerve alerts the brain thus preventing obesity but when the vagus nerve is not healed, it diverts the signals and they never reach the brain which ultimately causes obesity.

3) **Gastroparesis:**

The wellness of the digestive tract is one of the major part vagus nerve plays a pivotal role in. It keeps any problem to occur in that area of the human body but problem arises when the vagus nerve itself has trouble functioning well. Then occurs a disease known as gastroparesis which leads to the coercive contraction of the digestive system which makes the food last longer in the stomach. This results in the problems in excretion since the stomach have trouble emptying due to the contractions.

4) Dysphagia:

Dysphagia is a disease of the oesophagus where the patients have trouble swallowing certain food and when it is intense, the process of swallowing ceases entirely. There is no way the food goes in through the oesophagus then. Now, the fact is that the vagus nerve is responsible for taking care of the muscles that help the food to be swallowed through the oesophagus which halts all at once when the vagus nerve is damaged. The dysphagia occurs and there is no counteract from the vagus nerve.

5) Parkinson's disease:

The X cranial nerve is famous to provide the gut-brain axis. Hence, it helps the brain keep track of what's going on in the gut. In Parkinson's disease, the degeneration of brain occurs where the human body has problems in the movement, the Parkinson's disease births in the gut and finally, through the vagus nerve, which is a superhighway of the gut to the brain, travels to the brain when the vagus nerve is damaged and is not in the right state to function well. That makes matters worse, the disease then easily spreads through the brain without the vagus nerve alerting it and cause the degeneration of the brain.

6) Vasovagal Syncope:

This disease, also known as the fainting spell, is a result of damaged vagus nerve as discussed earlier. The X cranial nerve stimulates the muscles that are responsible for regulating the heart rate and the blood pressure level but when the damage occurs, the vagus nerve is overstimulated resulting in the vasovagal syncope where the vagus nerve overreacts to certain stress triggers.

Where breathing goes haywire and the person ends up fainting.

7) Cardiovascular disease:

The X cranial nerve activation is responsible for stabilizing the autonomic function and cardiovascular function which regulate the electromechanical function of the heart. Therefore, when the vagus nerve stops working well, the autonomic imbalance occurs stopping the sympathetic and parasympathetic systems from working on a regular pace. This increases the chances of heart failure or stroke. Don't just dismiss the fact that you have a proper working vagus nerve because it is one of the things you should be thankful for.

8) Postural orthostatic tachycardia syndrome (POTS):

The Postural orthostatic tachycardia syndrome is a disease which causes the person to have abnormal heart beat due to even the slightest of movements that involve lying down, standing up, walking a little and other day to day, easy tasks. The person experiences increased heart rate and breathlessness. The cause of the POTS is the dysfunction of the vagus nerve which occurs when a person faces cervical instability during any disease. This cause the vagus nerve to be compressed hence, damaged. This prevents the vagus nerve from transmitting the information, "You need to repair!" to the brain which causes heart beat to skyrocket even when the person just lifts their hand.

9) Mast Cell Activation Syndrome (MCAS):

The MCAS is a condition that results in hives, severe diarrhea, low blood pressure, breathing problems and swelling. This all is due to the compression of the vagus nerve yet again due to the cervical instability. The vagus nerve fails to send signals to the brain and the brain fails to identify the problem in order to work on it. The ligaments in the nape of the neck are loosened that cause the cervical instability, to tighten them is to prevent the compression of the vagus nerve.

10) Leaky Gut Syndrome:

Leaky gut syndrome refers to the condition when a person ends up having holes in the intestinal track lining and increases intestinal permeability. This provides all the toxins and bacteria lurking around a chance to invade the intestinal wall and cause immune system destruction. All of this once again is caused by the vagus nerve dysfunction. Next time you tell someone to take care, make sure you speak it like this instead: "Take care of your vagus nerve!" Sounds funny but didn't you see? Any harm to your vagus system can make you fall mad sick and nobody wants that.

11) Anxiety:

The anxiety is triggered by some event or a happening which human mind displeases. And the vagus nerve then comes to the rescue. It tells the brain to order the heart to relax and let the human being breath. But this all stops when the vagus nerve is not available to function well; or when it fails to get activated. This keeps the brain from causing the anxiety from strengthening its roots. Vagus nerve, is the manager of our brains, if it is unavailable, a lot of body organs get affected. Clearly in a bad way!

12) Attention deficit hyperactivity disorder (ADHD):

This very condition is often termed as mental disorder where the teens, adults or even the young kids perform involuntary acts and fail to control their impulses. The patients usually have aggressive behaviour which is the bone of contention and the most power nerve, the X cranial nerve helps control it. Therefore, when the vagus nerve is either damaged or removed, the vagus nerve stops making the substance which controlled the aggressive behaviour of the one affected. The ADHD then spreads like a wildfire.

13) Depression:

Depression is a very common condition that is found almost in every 8 out of 10 people. This soars high when the vagus nerve, the main actor which when gets activated, combats it, is damaged. Imagine your pizza delivery guy gets in an accident and has to go to the hospital, wouldn't it be worrisome? He would be injured and your pizza would never be delivered. Similarly, when the vagus nerve is damaged, the signals it delivers to the brain are lost somewhere and it fails to stop diseases like depression from rising.

14) Fibromyalgia:

This disease refers to musculoskeletal pain which results in fatigue, memory loss, mood changes and other sleep issues that keep the person up at night and sleeping at the odd hours of the day. Just as you expected, the vagus nerve dysfunction is behind this disease which disrupts the human biological clock. The vagus nerve fails to give brain the pain signals which is the information it needs to work on the organs hence, halting the complete process. So much work and just a pair of nerves! Aren't you left stupefied?

15) Food Sensitivities:

Food allergies or food sensitivities are caused by low vagal tone since the vagus nerve plays a major role in the wellness of our bodies. The food allergies occur when the vagal tone is reduced and brain doesn't get signals to tolerate any food you eat which results in food allergies.

16) Tinnitus:

The tinnitus is a condition involving ringing in ears and loss of hearing at times. It is due to the process where neurons in the brains get hyperactive which is caused by the vagus nerve dysfunction where the brain doesn't get any information from the vagus nerve to relax and heal.

17) Chronic Inflammation:

The part of the body where the inflammation occurs go through frequent changes in cells present there. The cells begin to damage and the vagus nerve while itself damage fails to alert the brain to carry out healing command which ends up strengthening the inflammation.

18) Sleep dysfunction:

The vagus nerve is concerned with dealing with insomnia and unhealthy sleep patterns. It allows the brain to calm down and find sleep easily once the chaos in the head subside. The vagus nerve sends signals to the brain which commands the sleep to come running but since it all stops the sleep seems to wander wherever it wants to come back when it desires.

19) Crohn's disease:

The Crohn's disease causes a lot of body organs to dysfunction. People fall badly ill once the Crohn's disease strikes but vagus nerve, the superhero comes to the rescue. Ever wondered what would happen if the vagus nerve gets damaged? Well, the Crohn's disease would never be cured because the only key to unlock the lock to good health is the X cranial nerve which is when damaged can never let you have a healthy life.

20) Irritable Bowel Syndrome (IBS):

The irritable bowel syndrome refers to the disease where the large intestine where abdominal pain, bloating, constipation or diarrhea, gas and cramps occur. The person also feels depressed when hit with this disease. The vagus nerve deals with the problems that occur in the digestive tract and when it gets compressed or damaged and shows dysfunction, the diseases like IBS occur.

21) Post-traumatic Stress Disorder (PTSD):

This mental disorder is one of the clingiest one. This refers to a mental condition which people witness after a shocking, terrifying or any dangerous event. The trauma strikes and stick to them like a second skin. There are certain events that end up triggering the stress which cause the person to have flashbacks, anxiety, nightmares, untamed thoughts regarding what they experienced. The vagus nerve has the tendency to deal with these problems which when damages, halts the PTSD prevention.

22) Alzheimer's disease:

The vagus nerve helps sharpen the memory by signalling the brain which prevents Alzheimer's from creeping in. The vagus nerve gets activated in no time when the person needs it to be stimulated and spread its magic everywhere but when it is damaged, the magic dies and the person becomes prone to let new and severe diseases invade their body. No choice there!

23) Roemheld Syndrome:

The Roemheld Syndrome is the condition where changes in gut occur. The intestinal gas and gastrointestinal issues keep attacking which result in tachycardia and arrhythmias which are the heart problems. The vagus nerve when damages, abstains from sending brain the signals which cause the brain to carry out the healing command. Therefore, when the gut has issues, the autonomic reflexes are activated resulting in the problems in the heart such as either painfully slow or incredibly fast heart rate and blood pressure.

24) Impaired immune system:

Due to vagus nerve dysfunction, a person's immune system is often impaired. An impaired immune system refers to a weak immune system that does not efficiently protect a human body against any disease unlike it usually does as a second line of defence it is. It makes the person prone to have HIV, AIDS and other fatal diseases. The vagus nerve is the super highway which provides other organs a way to communicate with the brain but when it is damaged, blocked or compressed, it causes the immune system to become the impaired immune system, fraught with fear of dangerous infections.

25) Bradycardia and Tachycardia:

As mentioned quadruple times, the vagus nerve is responsible to keep the heart rate in check but when it is damages, it causes the heart rate to go down the drain and slow down which results in bradycardia. Similarly, the tachycardia occurs when the heart rate is too high; that is yet again caused by vagus nerve dysfunction.

26) Sepsis:

It is recorded that 250,000 Americans die from sepsis each year. It is one of the deadliest diseases the vagus nerve keeps at bay but when the vagus nerve damages, it clears the coast for the sepsis to attack and make the human body vulnerable by stopping the chemicals to be released in the blood that fight all the infections and letting certain changes occur in the body which let so many organs to be damaged.

27) Postoperative Ileus:

Postoperative ileus or POI is an intestinal problem which causes the impairment of bowel or intestinal motility which causes severe pain in the abdomen. The vagus nerve dysfunction can cause this very problem to birth in people whereas the perfect vagus nerve prevents it.

28) Cluster headaches:

Cluster headaches are recurrent, excruciating headaches that occur in cycles and usually affect one side of the head. This is caused by misbalanced routine (that we all have) which affects the biological clock of the human being. The vagus nerve help fight this neurological disease by alarming the brain and letting it carry out a response to the pain which lessens it. But you can imagine what would happen if the vagus nerve dysfunction occurs. It would give way to cluster headaches and all the other pains that no entity would really want or like.

29) **B12 Deficiency:**

There are parietal cells in the gut which run well when the vagus nerve is stimulated properly but when it refrains from working properly, the problem arises known as vitamin B12 deficiency and the patients experience chronic digestive problems then. This is due to the low intrinsic factor, which is a chemical that processes the B12 in the stomach and all this happens due to unbalanced vagal tone index. The brain usually needs a signal from the vagus nerve which it fails to transmit which causes the stomach to refrain from produce the vitamin B12 and that, my friend, is the bone of contention. You ask why? It's because low B12 causes anxiety, chronic fatigue, depression, dementia and other memory problems. The vitamin B12 deficiency is one of the very common problems people from face all around the world and people often take time identifying it and then getting it diagnosed.

CHAPTER 4. HOW PAIN, STRESS AND ANXIETY AFFECT YOUR LIFE

How pain affects your life

At least 100 million Americans, or one in three, live with chronic pain. It's a debilitating condition that affects your ability to work, exercise, focus, relax, do basic household tasks, get a good night's sleep, and fully enjoy life.

Pain can affect your life in numerous ways. If you are a professional and have to go to work, if you experience pain, your work is affected. You will not be able to concentrate on finishing your tasks if something is wrong with you. If you are sick, you have to be absent for treatment or rest. Either way, your work is still affected. If you are a parent, how can you take care of your kids if you are hurt? Pain, is of course a natural stimulus that should not be taken for granted. The more you ignore the pain, the worse your situation may become.

If pain is chronic, it has a detrimental effect on the everyday life of the person. It affects the patient's ability to perform natural functions and responsibilities. Physical activities are limited.

Chronic pain affects you physically and psychologically. It limits what you can do. It interferes with your ability to work, play with your children or grandchildren; it also diminishes your ability to take care of your own self. When these happen, pain causes you to feel useless and incompetent, making you succumb to a depressed state. People with chronic pain often experience irritability, anger, depression, and difficulty in concentrating. It becomes as debilitating as the pain itself.

It pressures the person while he is trying to hide the pain and forces himself to cover the handicap by a sense of forged well-being to be functional.

Chronic pain is unpredictable. It is sometimes mild and other times, it is unbearable. When a person is in pain, his perception about things is obscured and his responses are slow. This is the stage where a person's personality does not reflect on the outside.

Pain causes sleeplessness and mood swings. Chronic pain leads to painful depressions and helplessness which, in turn leads to suicidal tendencies, anxiety and panic disorders.

If you're in chronic pain, do you notice the effects that it has on your mood and ability to live a normal life? If you have a loved one who suffers from chronic pain, have you noticed changes in them since their pain began?

Chronic pain has become a large-scale public health issue that dramatically worsens quality of life for many people and creates a sizable and growing financial drain on our health care system. The core of the issue is that the medical community does not know how to address the underlying cause of most chronic musculoskeletal pain. Why are drugs and surgery, which are effective roughly 50% of the time, their go-to treatments? The answer that "these are the best solutions we have" is simply not good enough anymore.

People who are in painful situations are always misunderstood. Oftentimes, their real perception and intentions are not reflected on the outside. Their ways of coping with pain is essentially vital to how people view them. Their view of life is also affected. Those who suffer from serious illnesses perceive life as something they have to live to the fullest as their time is already counted and the likes. Some also become hopeless and afraid of the things to come.

To shift out of the surgery-focused trend, some big changes are necessary. Doctors must be educated about the effectiveness of preventive care compared to surgery, and communicate this to their patients. Insurance companies must start covering more types of preventive care. And as a patient, you need to do your part by educating yourself about your condition and getting opinions from multiple doctors. You should also recognize that in many cases there are no magic pills or surgeries that will cure your pain forever. You must put in the work required to take care of yourself on a daily basis so that you can get out of and stay out of pain.

Imaging studies show that regions of the brain involved in making emotional decisions are also involved in chronic pain. To explore this connection, researchers at Northwestern University Medical School and SUNY Upstate Medical University paired chronic back pain patients with healthy control subjects on the Iowa Gambling Task, a card game that measures emotional decision-making abilities. The chronic pain patients performed poorly compared to the control subjects, showing the negative impact chronic pain has on your ability to make decisions.

Another major challenge is that people suffering from chronic pain tend to feel like they have no understanding or control over their pain. Despite all that modern medicine knows about the human body, the medical community still understands relatively little about pain—so much so that 85% of lower back pain sufferers receive no definitive diagnosis.

How Stress and Anxiety Affects Your body and Life

There can be situations when you just cannot act like before you used to because now anxiety has taken a grip of you. It is the feeling of being afraid of the unknown. On a broader sense, anxiety comes in different forms sometimes feeling worried, apprehensive, being nervous or plainly everything going out of control. Severe forms of anxiety can be extremely devastating and can have a great impact on your life and health.

Fear and panic are natural human emotions. Everyone has felt anxious for one reason or another. It is the feeling of worry, apprehension or panic in response to certain situations which is usually unsafe or uncomfortable.

Anxiety is a basic human emotion. Generally speaking, it is healthy and manageable to a certain degree.

Because everyone experiences anxiety, it can be challenging to recognize and accept anxiety as a problem, however if you just ignore the symptoms of anxiety, you miss the chance to understand your life and yourself better. If you try to understand what your anxiety is telling you, you will have a better chance of overcoming the problem. In effect, you get to enjoy a better quality of life.

Is your anxiety helping you or has it become excessive and detrimental? We'll now try to learn more about anxiety and what you can do to help control the problem.

There are several 'listed' disorders that are all classified as 'anxiety.' Depending on the duration of the anxiety and its severity, it can actually lead to physical symptoms. When it manifests physically, it can cause the person to feel worn out, rundown, fatigued, it can cause pain in muscles and joints, it can lead to an increased risk of getting sick, and it can even increase the risk of heart attack, stroke, and a number of other health emergencies.

There are probably plenty of things that you have gone through in your life that caused you some level of worry. Maybe you had a test in high school that worried you. Even if you studied and felt confident that you knew the material, you might have worried about that test.

Maybe it kept you from getting a good night's sleep right before that test. Would that be considered anxiety?

It all depends. Since it interfered with your ability to sleep, some people could have been diagnosed as having mild anxiety. But most likely once the test was over you were able to get back to your normal routine and didn't worry about it anymore, and that wouldn't be classified as anxiety. More like stress.

We all experience stress throughout our life. It's quite natural and normal, but when you begin to worry excessively about certain things, especially things that you cannot control, then it becomes a problem.

As you deal with stress on a regular basis, whether it's because of financial pressures, schooling, relationship problems, worries about your job or finding work, or anything else, it can develop into anxiety over time.

What usually happens is that the worry starts to consume your thoughts. You begin thinking about the challenges you're facing on a regular basis. You could be thinking about the rent that's late while driving home from work knowing you can't possibly pay it right now.

You could be worried about the company you work for downsizing. You might be concerned about your adult child's well-being because he's out partying every night, doesn't seem to be taking any responsibility for his life, is getting himself into debt, and nothing you say or do – aside from paying those bills for him-is making a difference.

When you try to fall asleep at night, when the TV is off and everything is quiet, you can't shut the worry and stress off. You keep turning those fears over and over in your mind.

At some point in the middle of the night you might finally drift off to sleep but the alarm blares just two or three hours later. Now you're tired and have the deal with another day like that.

Multiply that night after night and the anxiety will continue to build even more because now you're trying to focus at work, impress the boss, or getting impatient with people around you.

You might snap at somebody then feel bad about it right away, and that's going to make things worse in your mind. Eventually you may feel tightness in your chest, shortness of breath at times, and have a difficult time getting anything done.

Over time you might withdraw from some of the activities you used to enjoy because you're spending all of your time worrying about everything, even though you're not actually able to do anything about them.

In time, you're living a completely different life with little to enjoy. That can lead to depression and a general state of worry about many other things, even those things that weren't a major concern for you in the past.

Finding a way that helps us to deal with worries with less anxiety is the way to live better and accept the challenges that life throws at us one at a time without pre-occupying ourselves with them. our balance and wellbeing are fundamental to how we can best deal with the challenges we will face.

CHAPTER 5. POLYVAGAL THEORY

Introduced by Dr. Stephen Porges (Director at Brain-Body Center, University of Illinois, Chicago), The Polyvagal Theory helps us understand the correlation between the Vagus nerve and the body's autonomic reactions to different circumstances. It categorizes the functions of the two distinct branches constituting the nerve, namely the ventral and the dorsal branch, and states that when danger is perceived, the nervous system employs a series of strategies in a hierarchical manner, in order to overcome the situation.

A more evolved nervous system—like in the case of mammals—would make use of a significantly modified system of responses against any complexity. It includes augmented behavior and social engagement and is controlled by the ventral vagal complex.

The dorsal vagal complex, which is present in most vertebrates, causes an animal to freeze when facing a situation of great stress. It helps them in conserving their metabolic resources and opt for a fight or flight strategy. In evolved animals, this branch of the Vagus nerve takes over when social behavior is of no help in that particular instance.

Healing the Vagus nerve can assist in dealing with traumatic and stressful situations by regulating the nervous system's response to challenges, bringing about a state of calmness.

The Three Circuits of The Autonomic Nervous System

There are two primary nervous systems in your body, your peripheral nervous system, or PNS, and your central nervous system, or CNS.

The CNS is your spinal cord and brain. It controls thoughts. The PNS is all the other nerves, as well as ganglia. These regulate the limbs, organs, and muscles.

The PNS is the autonomic nervous system, or ANS, and the somatic nervous system. Both are responsible for involuntary and voluntary functioning. For example, you are talking, seeing, smelling, as well as digesting and breathing. Then the ANS is broken down into the parasympathetic and sympathetic nervous system. This is the "fight, flight, or freeze" impulse and "rest and digest."

When you relax and let yourself be calm, you signal your parasympathetic nervous system to "rest and digest." But if you become afraid or stressed, you have a physiological response. This is your sympathetic nervous system, or your "fight, flight, or freeze" response. Your body is responding to mobilize and handle the "threat." Your heart beats faster, and pupils dilate saliva production increases and your blood sugar increases.

When you are threatened or afraid, the model is fairly straightforward. Your body responds to a problem. For instance, is there always either a parasympathetic response or a sympathetic response, or can you operate without one of those responses? How does the body respond when the body is chronically stressed? Why does a body trigger the "fight, flight, or freeze" response when you see something dramatic on television when you know it is not real or is not life-threatening. Are emotions necessary for these responses?

Humans are “hard-wired” to be social and in groups. This means that social engagement is entangled with how you respond physiologically. This has led to humans coping with stressors that are urgent and impactful on the immediate self but also stressors that are social in nature, too. This theory, the polyvagal theory, attempts to stitch together factors of these such responses on a social, physiological, and evolutionary platform. But before getting into these factors, it is good to have a review of the Vagus nerve and how it deals with the regulation of your stress levels.

CHAPTER 6. THE HEALING POWER OF THE POLYVAGAL THEORY

Part of the Polyvagal Theory explored earlier in this book, is what some people call the "social nerve system." Dr. Stephen Porges developed this concept, going on to describe how the social nerve system is a portion of the brain where the eyes, voice, and facial expressions are influenced and are used to influence others.

The reason babies are so often used as examples for this theory is that human babies are born helpless. They need protection and support as they continue to develop. Because they cannot walk or talk, the infant human body adapted with skills designed to activate the social nerve system in the adult. While modern science may still only recognize or discuss two nervous systems, the sympathetic and parasympathetic, there is a third that needs to be injected into the system that offers an explanation to the gaps that still exist when it is just the two polarities. Each one of the systems is designed to deal with stress in a different manner.

For example, think of an infant who shifts its body to face toward their parent, and uses their eyes and facial gestures to signal his or her parents. If this fails and no one acknowledges the message she or he is trying to send, the parasympathetic nervous system is activated and the infant begins to get angry and cry. And if this message still goes unanswered, the infant can then "play dead," becoming quiet and still. As the infant learns how the different responses and strategies work, the more it becomes ingrained in their subconscious and used as they grow into an adult.

This third system, the social nervous system, makes sense. The entire body and mind, including your nervous system, seeks balance inside and out. It wants to not only be harmonious in its internal functioning, but it also wants to feel harmonious with its surroundings. This is why, when your life is stressful and "stormy," you probably have a natural tendency or inclination to reach out to someone to find empathy. You want or even need to share with others because it is important for your survival to know that you are not alone and that what you are going through is not just a "you" thing or something that sets you apart from the rest. With this information now in your "tool belt," you may feel like a fog has dissipated and you can finally see yourself and others more clearly now.

Now that you know the social nervous system and the three systems and responses, you can recognize the stage a person is in. Not only does this help you, but it helps you see how other people are doing around you. Are they shutting down and "playing dead" because you or others have failed to acknowledge their needs? Or are they screaming for attention? Can you try and catch them when they are engaging their social nervous system and displaying the Polyvagal Theory in their facial expressions?

Your body and brain send out various energetic frequencies. Think about brain waves. These are like sound waves and are measurable frequencies. Researchers, such as Dr. Joe Dispenza, identified that infant brain waves are primal and connected to the development of the subconscious. During this time the subconscious is being developed and finalized with the important survival needs. It is developing a strategy to help you survive as you grow and later in life. When the infant reaches childhood, the brain waves and frequencies shift. They become more creative. Imagination and creative play, like turning an everyday object into a monster, dinosaur or horse. It is also why monsters live under the bed, etc.

These frequencies do not leave you when you become an adult, but often they become only active right before and just as you fall asleep. It is also common just when you wake up or when you are deep in meditation. These connections are very close to the subconscious. In these states, you have the ability to change the pattern of your neurology and "reprogram" what you learned as an infant and young child about survival among other things.

When you turn ten your brainwaves and energetic frequencies change again. Now they are more "mature" and follow a more rational approach. This change continues throughout adulthood. At this point the brain can identify the difference between different things, like the everyday object is not really a dinosaur and the shadow is just a shadow, not a monster. In addition, it provides the ability to rationalize emotions and situations. For example, you can find a rational reason why you should not deal with your emotions.

But while you may convince your mind not to deal with it, eventually it will come out, and your body will respond in ways you cannot or do not want to control. You rationalize yourself into illness. At this point, you have learned about the various stages of brain and energy waves, as well as the three nervous systems; social, sympathetic, and parasympathetic. You have also been introduced to the idea that the way adults respond to stressful situations is due to the strategies they found which worked best for them when they were children. From a neuroscience point of view, this information is transformational. This information shows that the immune system, endocrine, and nervous system are all connected and working together inside you.

The concept is basic; if you are socially unable to cope with your stress, the body then begins to "fight, flight, or freeze." This physiological state is not a place you want or should stay in long. If you do not cope with this threat or stress quickly, your body and mind start to fade. How you choose to interact with others includes the degree of interaction as well as the manner of contact. This determines the majority of your health. To find this balance and harmony, you need to do more than just meditate for 15 minutes every day by yourself or do a 30-minute relaxation yoga video by yourself. Therefore the third system, the social nervous system, regulated largely by the Vagus nerve, supports your need to connect. Think about the importance of going to church on a Saturday or Sunday. You can pray at home, but it is important to be together with others that support your view on spirituality. It is also why going to a fitness class is a far different outcome, especially on your happiness, than doing a program at the house by yourself. This means it is not about the actions physically, but about the connection socially. Studies at this stage people's brain waves become calmer and more peaceful. And all this knowledge then leads to a powerful change agent you can use in your future.

CHAPTER 7. VAGUS NERVE ACTIVATION

Now, with the vagus nerve being so integral to so much of the body's functions, you may wonder what exactly can be done in order to actively treat these problems when they do arise. After all, wouldn't activating the vagus nerve be the best treatment when you are seeing that your symptoms are directly related to having an underactive nerve?

You can trigger your vagus nerve when necessary. You can use vagus nerve activation and stimulation to trigger it to do something to help you self-regulate. If you know that you are being anxious, you can trigger that stimulation via deep breathing. If you know that your anger is related to your inability to get out of the fight or flight response, you can trigger that vagus nerve in order to trigger your body to relax.

Effectively, then, *your vagus nerve is like a tiny little button* that you have—a switch that you can flip when you know that you need a little boost in calm. You can use methods of vagus nerve stimulation to trigger that parasympathetic nervous system so you can, in fact, stop the fight-flight-freeze response. If you have that little switch, why wouldn't you go out of your way to make use of it? Why would anyone choose not to take advantage of the fact that they can actively self-regulate like that?

Why Activate the Vagus Nerve?

Way back in 1921, inspired by a dream, scientist Otto Loewi attempted an experiment. After a period in trying to figure out whether nerves were able to communicate through either chemical or electrical impulses, Loewi had an idea. He performed vivisection on two frogs next to each other—in one, he severed the vagus nerve. In the other, he left the heart connected to the nerve. He then stimulated the vagus nerve of the frog still attached to it and bathed the heart in saline solution as the heart slowed down. In spreading that same saline solution to the frog with the detached nerve, it was found that the heart rate still slowed down. Thus, it became clear that the vagus nerve could chemically communicate with the heart, slowing it down via neurotransmitters.

In activating the vagus nerve, the heart rate was slowed, but it did more than that —it also makes it clear that the vagus nerve is able to impact far more than just the heart if the vagus nerve is stimulated triggered all sorts of various neurotransmitters that inevitably traveled beyond just the heart. This means that activating the nerve would then create the stimulation necessary to impact all sorts of areas within the body.

This means, then, that you can activate your own vagus nerve to get yourself to calm down. You can use the vagus nerve to effectively impact several areas of your body all at once. The vagus nerve and stimulating it, then, becomes something critical if you want to treat any of the typical issues associated with a problem with the vagus nerve.

How to Stimulate the Vagus Nerve

Electrical stimulation of the vagus nerve is commonly done with a device known as a vagal nerve stimulator (VNS) device. Because it becomes clear that there are several different benefits to stimulating the vagus nerve, scientists have figured out how to effectively trigger the vagus nerve at will. Using a device that is meant to send a short electrical impulse into the nerve in order to trigger its activation, the vagus nerve can be stimulated.

Developed in the 1980s, the VNS was found to treat seizures in epilepsy patients. It was installed within the body, attached to the vagus nerve, and is free to zap the nerve whenever necessary. Acting sort of like a pacemaker, it sends regular impulses up to the brain. This makes it a valuable device to help mitigate epilepsy and other disorders, effectively allowing for the regular electrical impulses to be sent to the brain. This then makes it, so the people who are needing the trigger can do so as needed.

This device was monumental—while it did not cure epilepsy by any means, it did allow for the regulation of the seizures, and in some cases, did lead to a decrease in the seizure activity that people had. However, this is quite invasive—it requires attaching a device that can potentially fail to a nerve that is designed to regulate just about everything about you that will keep you alive.

Vagus Nerve Stimulation at Home

Of course, there is always the option of using vagal nerve stimulation at home through various means. You can activate your vagus nerve at home through all sorts of methods ranging from deep breaths to singing, to even attempting to use a coffee enema. No matter the method that you choose, you get one major benefit from doing so at home as opposed to having a device implanted: It is noninvasive.

When you stimulate your vagus nerve at home, you can develop all sorts of methods that can be used to actively trigger your nerve without anyone around you knowing any better. Even just taking deep breaths can be done discreetly without those around you, realizing that you are actively attempting to trigger the use of it. When you do this, you can effectively allow yourself a sort of life preserver. If you are having an anxiety attack, you can use breathing to stimulate your vagus nerve. If you commonly suffer from inflammation or inflammatory issues, you may make it a point to use these methods to better protect yourself as well.

Ultimately, as you read through the next chapters, you will learn exactly how to trigger your vagus nerve in a wide range of settings and contexts. In doing so, you will build up an arsenal of techniques that will greatly benefit you.

What Can You Treat Through Vagus Nerve Activation?

The vagus nerve travels practically throughout the body, and because of that, it can influence a wide range of the body as well. In particular, it travels down the neck, into the abdomen, and branches out to touch other nerves within the peripheral nervous system. It reaches down to the colon, and in doing so, it is believed that about 90% of the body's afferent nerves—nerves that are designed to send information from the body back up to the brain—will contact the vagus nerve and use the vagus nerve to transmit information.

In doing so, it makes several important stops. In fact, it can directly interact with areas related to:

- The heart: At this point, we have already emphasized just how much the vagus nerve connects to the heart. In fact, it is necessary to be able to slow down the heart, particularly after an event that has activated the sympathetic nervous system. The vagus nerve releases acetylcholine, which allows for the slowing of the pulse and drop of blood pressure.
- The lungs: Along the way, the vagus nerve also interacts with the lungs. Thanks to the fact that the heart and lungs are so closely intertwined, it makes sense that they would directly impact each other. The vagus nerve is involved in

constricting bronchi within the lungs—it effectively makes breathing a bit more difficult.

- The digestive system: The vagus nerve makes it all the way throughout the digestive system as well. Remember, the parasympathetic nervous system, part of what the vagus nerve controls, is rooted in rest-and-digest mode. This means that the vagus nerve must be regularly active if it is going to be able to digest properly. When not properly stimulated, it can lead to all sorts of digestive issues.
- Inflammation: Interestingly, the vagus nerve is also related to the response meant to regulate inflammation. When the body is injured or fighting off an infection, it creates inflammation. The vagus nerve is necessary to

pass the message that the injury requires inflammation so the spleen can trigger the inflammatory response. The vagus nerve then is involved in also canceling that response—it tells the brain to stop the inflammation as well.

- Relaxation: The vagus nerve directly controls your ability to relax. Through the release of acetylcholine to activate the parasympathetic nervous system, the vagus nerve also triggers the activation of that relaxation response. It is also capable of triggering oxytocin, vasopressin, and prolactin, all of which are closely related to reward and reproductive systems.
- Memories: The vagus nerve functioning improperly can also cause the body to struggle with creating memories in a proper manner.

In stimulating the vagus nerve, norepinephrine is released into the amygdala, the part of the brain that helps with memory storage.

1.Physical Activity

Exercise is a necessary part of healing from chronic pain. You don't have to become an active bodybuilder or an athlete, but some degree of body movement is highly desirable to prevent chronic pain. Body movements release the "stuck" energy in our body and ensure a smooth flow of energy to prevent any pain.

Exercising is a great way to reduce your anxiety. Whether you wake up earlier in the morning before you have to go to work and go for a run, or if you can go when you get home from and jog around the block.

Also, if you do exercise more this will help with your self-esteem. Exercising will make you healthier and you will feel better about yourself. If you are worried about your health and it is making your anxiety worse, get out there and do some exercises. You don't even have to leave your house; you could just find an exercise DVD and start doing some exercise from your own living room. To really help lower anxiety, it is a good idea that each time you exercise to be sure it is for 30 minutes or more. Studies have shown that it takes about thirty minutes for your anxiety to lower when exercising.

If you don't want to exercise alone, grab a friend to do this activity with you. This will make you happy and you can have someone to talk to about the things you are anxious about. It's great to have someone who you can let all of your feelings be expressed to who can help you. Healthy exercise has some surprising implications for those with anxiety disorders and other psychological conditions including depression. The mechanisms by which exercise, and mental health are related are not fully understood, but many medical experts around the world now acknowledge that exercise has a major impact on a wide range of psychological conditions. It is even now believed that exercise can be as effective at combating depression as many commonly prescribed drugs.

Short bursts of activity a few times a day are the type of exercise that experts recommend. A brisk walk lasting only ten minutes is believed to be enough to raise your emotional state for a couple of hours. For those with anxiety disorders, it can be hard to get out and about on occasion. For some, with severe conditions, it can seem impossible. Exercise, however, will really help to improve your emotional state and take your mind off anxiety. Use the following tips to increase your chances of successfully incorporating exercise into your life.

Moderate level intensity exercise is recommended as perfect for improving your physical health and also your mental health. This includes; walking briskly, cycling, jogging or swimming. Walking and jogging should not need any investment and if you're uncomfortable alone, partner up with a friend or relative. Ideally buddy up with someone who is addressing the same issues or has a good understanding of them, for extra support.

When we exercise, the brain releases endorphins, or “feel good” chemicals that are responsible for the “high” that many people feel during and after exercise. Another benefit of exercise for those with depression is that it lends purpose and structure to each day. Outdoor exercise has been shown to be especially effective for lifting mood.

Regular exercise can help maintain a healthy weight, which can be a problem in depressed people. Exercise promotes overall wellbeing, including heart health and a toned, more muscular body. The weight-bearing aspects of exercise prevent the body from losing bone mass and decrease the risk of osteoporosis, a particular benefit for women.

People who suffer from anxiety may not be interested in exercise. When someone is overwhelmed by the stress of everyday life, working out seems less than appealing. However, research shows that exercise plays an important role in reducing anxiety symptoms.

While exercise has been clinically proven to reduce anxiety and improve mood, it can also treat a number of other health problems. Health issues can be a major anxiety trigger, and easing the symptoms of those ailments can reduce anxiety symptoms further.

In addition, exercising can help people relax. When a person exercises, their body releases hormones that produce a calming effect. Exercise also increases body temperature, which can be very relaxing. Working up a sweat is tiring, but it's a great way to calm down.

Speed Walking

Speed walking, more often referred to as power walking or race walking, is a technique of walking at a rapid pace. Walking is a great alternative to running and is oftentimes much easier and more accessible to a greater variety of people. Walking provides all of the aerobic benefits of running while steering clear of many of the injuries associated with high-impact techniques of running. The activity of walking at an increased rate then walking "normally" can help participants lose weight, tone their muscles, and also increase their mood.

Not only is speed walking valuable for the muscles and joints, but it also reinforces overall health.

Stretching

Stretching is something everyone should do on a regular basis, and those with chronic back pain will benefit most from stretching the soft the muscles, ligaments, and tendons in and around the spine.

It is a fact that when motion is limited the back becomes stiff, which can result in more pain. Those who suffer from chronic back pain need to stretch regularly and perform appropriate stretching movements to benefit from the sustained and long-term relief from the increased motion.

One top recommendation for dealing with chronic pain is by getting regular exercise. Exercise will help with different types of pain - from helping with arthritis by getting your body moving, to boosting your mood, when you have pain from Crohn's disease or

fibromyalgia.

Yoga for Chronic Pain

Yoga can be defined as a practice based on harmonizing the mind, body, and soul. By practicing Yoga every day, you will not only explore your true self or your inner self, but also develop the feeling that you are one with nature and environment. Yoga aids the overall well-being of the body and focuses mainly on developing relationship with the natural world around us.

Pain is not just influenced by physical injury or illness, it is also greatly affected by our thoughts, anxiety, trauma, stress and emotions. Stress and pain are closely interrelated - you may experience pain when stressed and stress can also increase the intensity of the pain. When there is increased stress, your breathing becomes heavier, erratic and ragged. Your mood is also altered along with some tension and tightening of the muscles. These symptoms of chronic pain can even increase the toxins in the body and decrease oxygen levels.

Yoga addresses these problems effectively, as it involves the techniques of deep breathing and meditation, which helps in the absorption of much-needed oxygen and also in the relaxation of mind and body. These breathing techniques ensure that the muscles of the lungs, diaphragm, back, and abdomen are fully utilized. When the muscles are loose and relaxed, they can help in releasing the built-up tension in the body and facilitate proper flow of energy throughout. Stress and anxiety levels will also be reduced gradually.

Yoga, or simple stretching, are simple practices that should be applied to everyday life to reduce the tension of stress and keep the muscles in proper working order. There are specific stretches that can focus on problem areas such as the neck or lower back. These stretches can be assigned from a personal trainer, massage therapist, or physiotherapist. Yoga can be enjoyed at home or in a studio with several other participants. There are many forms of yoga ranging from hatha yoga to hot yoga. The focus in yoga is on breath control, meditation, stretching, and balance. Not all forms of yoga are spiritual with chants and mantras, if you don't feel comfortable with that form of practice.

Exercise in general is good for chronic pain, but specific exercises, especially certain yoga positions, help to decrease some types of pain, like shoulder or neck pain.

Additionally, the relaxation techniques you will learn, can teach you how to manage the different types of chronic pain more effectively.

If you are considering trying yoga techniques for your chronic pain, you need to consider the style of yoga you will do.

While all forms of yoga can be beneficial for your body, mind and spirit, certain exercises are directed towards people who are struggling with chronic pain.

There are multiple yoga poses or asanas and different stance can be used. Individuals with chronic pain should begin with a slow-paced, gentle yoga pose. Benefits of yoga include improved ability to handle stress, feeling more relaxed throughout the day and improvements in sleep quality. Studies have proven that yoga is helpful to prevent fibromyalgia, among other chronic pain conditions.

Tai Chi

Tai chi practice increases vagus nerve activity and reduces heart rate, blood pressure, blood glucose and cholesterol levels.

2.Massage Therapy

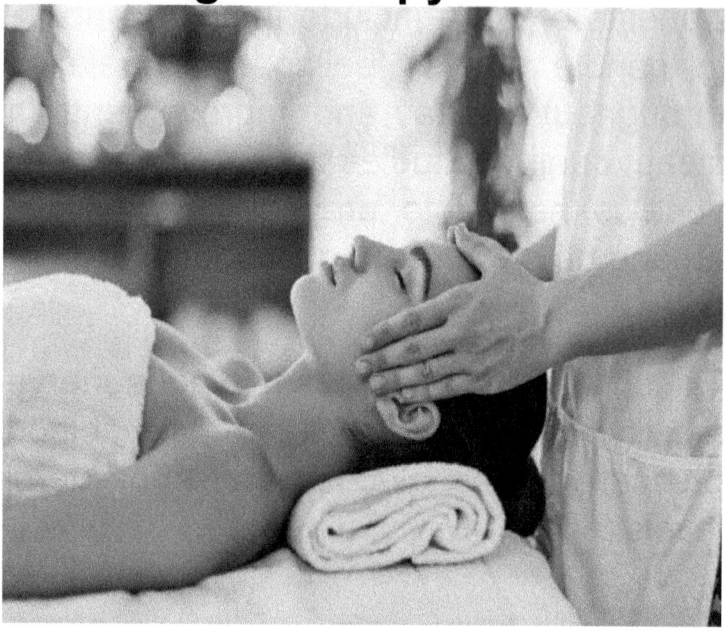

Massage therapy has become overwhelmingly popular, and rightfully so; in addition to feeling good, it has several health benefits. Massage therapy is wonderful for any type of pain, be it chronic, acute or simply from fatigue, work, and tension. There are various massage therapies available to meet all types of needs, including Shiatsu, Swedish, hot oil and deep tissue.

Massage has also been used as a natural anxiety remedy for ages; it may be as simple as rubbing your neck gently but whichever the case you are massaging it is an effective way to calm your nerves. The benefits of any massage therapy are many, including stress relief, relaxation, lowered blood pressure, lowered tension in the muscles, and it also improves deeper breathing. As the book unfolds, I will discuss therapeutic massage as a natural remedy for anxiety disorders, in this case it will be a deep and precise tool.

A skilled and trained massage therapist will know exactly what to do once the pain problem is explained. Massage also does wonders for fatigue and stress, both of which are known to increase pain and go hand in hand with arthritis and other chronic pain conditions. It can also help to calm anxiety, which often afflicts those who suffer from chronic pain.

If you can afford it, get a massage regularly - weekly or even twice per week. Physical therapists and chiropractors also offer therapeutic massage, so it may be covered under medical insurance.

There are also electronic massagers on the market that are great options. These include mobile units, which are spot massage products that target the neck or specific areas. There are also strap onto chair units that offer shiatsu for the entire back, many come with a heat option.

The most significant health benefit of massage is that it provides the sensation of touch, which is critical in both early childhood development and overall adult health. Levels of somatotropin, or human growth hormone, correlate directly with the amount of physical contact you receive.

Massage also cues relaxation in your nervous system. One of the biggest benefits of massage is that it feels great, especially if you're in pain. Nerves that carry information about the sensation of touch to the brain are more heavily myelinated than the nerves that carry information about pain, so touch information travels faster than pain information. This is why you instinctively rub the skin around a painful area; the touch sensation temporarily drowns out the pain sensation, and you're given a brief moment of relief.

Massage also feels good because it temporarily reduces muscle tension. Pressing on tight muscles lengthens them in the same way that gentle prolonged static stretching does, and after an hour or so of this manual lengthening you may stand up feeling like your muscles are made of jelly. If your massage therapist applies a great deal of pressure, your stretch reflex may be activated immediately, making you feel tight and sore soon after a massage. A good rule of thumb is that if you feel pain during a massage, you're probably going to feel some soreness afterward as well.

While it can be difficult or awkward in the moment, it's better to ask your massage therapist to press more gently than to suffer the consequences. It is absolutely not necessary to apply a painful amount of pressure to reap the benefits of a massage. Moreover, if you're in pain, a deep massage can increase and prolong your pain by making your muscles tighter.

Lastly, massage temporarily softens connective tissues, which increases flexibility and range of motion. Tendons, ligaments, fascia (which surrounds, supports, and separates structures of the body), and scar tissue (which forms to heal an injury) are all made of collagen fibers arranged in varying patterns and densities. As muscles become habitually tighter and movement decreases, connective tissues also respond by tightening. Movement and heat can make these collagen structures more flexible and fluid.

For people with chronic pain, the most beneficial aspect of massage may be that it lowers stress, thereby reducing the sensation of pain and reactivity of the nervous system. However, a massage by itself is not enough to change deeply learned habitual movements or your resting level of muscle tension. The sensory awareness that can be gained through massage is valuable, but if it isn't followed by actual motor education in the form of voluntary movement, little lasting progress will be made. You must actively retrain your nervous system, and you can't do that with massage alone.

3.Brain Balance

First, you must make sure your brain is balanced. Without a balanced nervous system, your efforts to eliminate chronic pain will be wasted. Many things can cause brain imbalances. Most common are head injuries and exposure to electromagnetic radiation from personal wireless devices. Things that increase brain imbalance risk factors include:

- Using Bluetooth devices and cell phones, walkie talkies, using desktop and laptop computers and iPads.
- Eating processed foods that have MSG.
- Consuming drinks containing artificial sweeteners, and

drinking fluoridated water.

- Leading a stressful life.
- Not getting enough quality sleep.

Brain Balancing Using Affirmations

Studies show that when the thymus gland is balanced, both hemispheres of the brain also remain balanced and serve to lower chronic pain. The nice thing about affirmations is that they don't cost you anything; you just have to repeat the affirmations regularly throughout the day to keep your brain in balance. You need to "feel" the words to get full benefits. The following is a list of daily affirmations:

- I have faith, gratitude, trust, love and courage.
- I'm modest, I'm humble and tolerant.
- I'm clean and good, I deserve to be loved.
- I'm content and tranquil.

- I have forgiveness in my heart.
- My life energy is high, life is full of love.

Brain Balancing Music

Brain balancing music encourages a balanced nervous system and balances both hemispheres of the brain. Brain balancing music uses three coordinated methods: “primordial sounds”, “brainwave entrainment”, and “multi-layered music” to bring the mind-body into a deeply relaxed and balanced state. You have to listen to the music on a daily basis to maintain your brain balance which is crucial for health and healing of chronic pain.

Avoid GMO foods

GMO or genetically modified organisms have been introduced to our diets over the past decade. As of this writing, the GMO foods are not labeled in the U. S. So, the average American’s is unconsciously consuming GMO rich canola oil, sugar. beets, corn, soy and cottonseed oil. GMO foods can cause all sorts of gastrointestinal problems, allergies, weight gain, and immune problems. Avoiding GMO foods can reduce or even eliminate many health problems, including chronic pain.

4.Prayer and Meditation

Prayer and meditation for even just 2-3 minutes have been proven to activate the vagus nerve and relieve anxiety and stress, with a general increase in relaxation.

5.Cold Exposure

When our bodies adapt to cold temperatures, the vagus nerve is activated to reduce the sympathetic stress response and increase the parasympathetic state of rest and relaxation. In addition to strengthening the vagus nerve, exposure to cold has the following benefits:

- Increasing lymph flow, which removes toxins, bacteria, viruses and other waste products from the body,

- Makes the heart pump more efficiently to increase blood flow and deliver more oxygen and nutrients to the whole body,

- increasing energy levels,

- speeding up our metabolism, which strengthens the immune system to fight infections and diseases.

Exposure to cold can be achieved thanks to:

- cold showers

- drinking cold water

- placing an ice pack on the forehead or sides of the neck

- spraying the face with cold water

- Sucking on an ice cube

- Eating popsicles

6.Acupressure and Acupuncture

Acupressure and acupuncture increase heart rate variability and activate the vagus nerve, helping to reduce inflammation, improve digestion and alleviate nausea and vomiting. There are 3 pressure points that specifically stimulate the vagus nerve

- Concha cymba - in the cavity above the ear canal.

- Stomach 36 - 3 fingers wide from the wrist, between the two large tendons.

- Nei Guan P6 - 4 fingers wide from the base of the kneecap, on the outside of the shin.

You can stimulate these vagus nerve acupressure points easily at home by applying firm but painless downward pressure with your thumb or finger in a circular motion for 1-2 minutes on each.

7.Gargling

Gargling activates the muscles in the back of the throat, through which the vagus nerve passes. Gargling to the point of tearing is recommended for effective activation of the vagus nerve. Dr Navaz Habib suggests doing this with warm salt water for effective action against bacteria in the back of the throat.

8.Humming/Singing

Humming or singing activates the vocal cords, through which the vagus nerve passes. Such stimulation increases the variability of the heart rate.

9.Eating Habits

OMEGA 3 FATS

Intake of omega-3 promotes activation of the vagus nerve and improves heart rate. These anti-inflammatory fats are found in

- fatty fish (salmon),

- linseed, which should be used sprouted for greater benefits

- chia seeds

- hemp seeds

- walnuts, (preferably activated ones)

HIGH FIBRE DIET

The habit of consuming fibre-rich foods - fruits, vegetables, nuts, seeds, whole grains, beans and legumes - is essential for regular bowel movements and consequently promote vagus nerve activation. Fibre has the added benefit of nourishing the good bacteria in the gut, reducing inflammation to the benefit of nerve activation itself.

PROBIOTICS

The vagus nerve innervates the gut. Probiotics and fermented foods increase the good bacteria in the gut, which activates the vagus nerve. 90% of the nerves from the gut connect to the brain via the vagus nerve. The increase in good bacteria in the gut has been shown to reduce anxiety, stress and depression.

Fermented foods includes:

- Sauerkraut
- Kimchi
- Ruby Kraut
- Beet Kvass
- Water kefir/Coconut milk kefir

CHAPTER 9. 5 MINUTE ROUTINE TO ACTIVE THE VAGUS NERVE

This exercise routine to stimulate the vagus nerve will help you rewire your brain whenever you should need it.
These exercises will allow you to relieve the symptoms of anxiety and stress, but also to feel more calm and relaxed at any time of the day. Today's life is full of challenges and commitments and anxiety is the normal response of our body to the hectic environment that surrounds us.

This practice is inspired by the book "Accessing the Healing Power of the Vagus Nerve" by Stanley Rosenberg, which details the Polyvagal Theory.
A necessary premise is that these exercises aim to make us feel better and should in no way be done with effort and tension. The movements must be soft and the body active but relaxed. Everyone will do it according to their physical condition and especially to their feeling. Let's always listen before starting

any practice or exercise.

First exercise: sit in a comfortable position (you can choose between a chair or the floor) with your hands along your hips. Put your right hand on top of your head and tilt your right ear towards your shoulder (the right one). This way you will be bent sideways to the right. At this point only move your eyes as the head will remain fixed in this position, while the eyes will go up and to the left. So the vision will no longer be front facing but moving to the left. Hold this position for 30 seconds.

Then release. Remember to listen to your body: you may notice a sigh, swallowing or breathing a little deeper than usual. Take a short break and proceed exactly in the same way on the left side of your body.

This simple exercise will prove to be valuable to dissolve tensions and feel more centered and present.

The time equal to 30 seconds is the minimum to get some beneficial effects however it can be prolonged in the event that you do not notice a sigh, a swallowing or any signal that tensions and rigidity have been unlocked.

Second exercise: this practice is focused on breaking any tension in the neck and relaxing all the muscles that concern it. The beneficial effects of this exercise involve the whole rib cage and it is there that we will focus to maximize the activation of the Vagus Nerve and its beneficial effects.

First bring your right hand to the top of the top of the head and then take your left hand and embrace the right side of the rib cage. Bring your head towards your right shoulder in a manner by bringing your right ear closer to your shoulder. At this point you bend to the right while the left hand pulls to the left. You should feel the ribs closing under your left hand and the whole spine will bend in the shape of a C. Now we repeat with our eyes the movement of exercise 1, that is, we look to the left and hold it for 30 seconds.

It's very important not to strain or exaggerate the movement. If it's not comfortable, it's better to make a less pronounced movement and then release.

At the end of this practice, you should note that breathing is a little easier.

Generally, it is not necessary to make great efforts or fatigue the important thing is to repeat these exercises constantly until you find relief and you feel better. As with any practice it is much more impactful to be consistent in practicing than to make great movements and few repetitions.

The same exercise should be performed in the same way on the other side of the body. It's important to respect your body and remember that each part has different tension and elasticity.

Third exercise: find a place to lie down comfortably and practice undisturbed. Face down, lie on your stomach and with your hands close to your chest (flat on the floor) stretch your elbows and raise your torso. Thus the shoulders should be supported by the elbows. At this point turn your head and look over your shoulder; you are lifting your head using the muscles along the side of your neck. Hold this position for 30 seconds. This helps to restore the SCM muscle that is the diseased muscle along the side of the neck. This can be useful for headaches or headache's tensions. Release. Do the same practice for the other side. Always for a minimum of 30 seconds and then release.

CHAPTER 10. BREATHING AND VAGUS NERVE

One way to naturally stimulate the vagus nerve is via breathing. Did you know the right kind of breathing helps immensely with stimulating the vagus nerve? How does that work though? Well, you'll find out here. Breathing, combined with meditation, or even on its own, is one of the best ways to stimulate your vagus nerve, and we'll tap into why that is, and how it helps in this chapter.

Why Breathing?

First, I want you to do an exercise. Sit down, close your eyes, and take a nice, deep breath in through the nose, noticing the belly expanding rather than the chest. From there, breathe out, and notice how the belly contracts.

Did you notice as you dd this how your body slowly relaxed, how your heart rate settled, and maybe you feel a little less anxious?

Well, that's an example of diaphragmic breathing, and how it stimulates the body.

Diaphragmic breathing, or deep breathing, is breathing with your diaphragm as the focus, rather than the chest. When you breathe from your chest, you're not supplying the body with oxygen-rich air, and many times, it will deprive the body of this. Breathing from your chest is how hyperventilation happens, and in some cases, brings about anxiety in some people.

When you breathe from your diaphragm, you'll feel it, and your body will naturally relax. That's because you're activating the parasympathetic nervous system. Most people discount this form of breathing to relieve stress, but it's very important not just for stress relief, but stimulating your vagus nerve.

When you do this though, you must understand that not all forms of breathing are equal. You have to breathe in through the nose, and from there, feel your belly expand. Sometimes, I like to hold my hand there in order to help facilitate the feeling of this. From there, I will notice how the stomach grows, and then fattens with this.

When you do this, you should notice your heart rate, breathing rate, and your body's general wellness change. Some people report a change in heart rate when that happens. Others will report a change in the way heir breathing occurs. Some people will also notice their bodies general relax over time. This is a type of breathing that can help you with improving vagal tone, since it's naturally touching on this, and it will help with stimulating your parasympathetic nervous system.

When you breathe quickly, that'll stimulate your sympathetic nervous system. That's important for physical activities but if you're always breathing that quickly, you'll force yourself into a panic attack. It gives the body the sign it has to be ready for action, whereas when you breathe in deeply, it'll naturally stimulate your vagus nerve, so it'll help with making sure that your body is taken care of, and that the vagus nerve is properly touched upon.

Deep breathing is essential to general health, wellness, and happiness.

Does Deep Breathing Help in Other Ways?

Of course! Deep breathing isn't just for vagus nerve stimulation. It helps with a lot of the various aspects of your body, and we'll talk a little bit here about how deep breathing helps you.

When you breathe in deeply, you'll provide more oxygen to the body. Oxygen is important, because it helps recover from hard exercises, and it also helps the body feel less stressed over time.

It reduces the exertion that's in the body, and it allows for you to get better sleep, and help stimulate creativity, and provide mental clarity as well. If you have brain fog happening, breathing deeply can help with this.

It also naturally relaxes the body. So, after a day filled with stress, it's the perfect means to help chill out after a very long day.

But, along with that is overall health. When you breathe in deeply, you're supplying oxygen to the body. That means, all physical activities within the body are better. It'll help with digestion, secretion, nervous system function, and also help with your heart rate.

It'll reduce the instances of vasovagal syncope, and also help with reducing inflammation in the body. It can boost immunity too, and red blood cell function.

Simply put, just by breathing in deeper, it'll help with improving your body's overall health. You'll start to feel the difference right away, and improve on these aspects too.

However, when you do deep breathing, you need to make sure that you're breathing with the whole body, and not just with your mouth. When you breathe from your mouth, you'll notice you'll feel less anxious. When you breathe from your diaphragm too, you'll stay more grounded, and you might even notice your diaphragm moving, and if you take your blood pressure, you'll notice as well it'll lower too.

In the body, diaphragmic breathing does other things too. When you breathe from the diaphragm, it triggers acetylcholine release, which helps with reducing stress in the body. It also reduces cortisol rates. Cortisol is the stress chemical, so in general, it'll promote the parasympathetic activity, and relaxation.

It also will take the inflammation system, so those with autoimmune disorders will notice the difference right away. It can reduce further inflammation, and also help with inflammation in the future too.

Your body will feel inner calmness. When you breathe from your diaphragm, it is controlled breathing. This gives you a sense of control over yourself, your emotions, and the adaptations that you have psychologically, and it'll allow you to express yourself better, and you'll notice you'll feel a lot calmer in even the worst of situations.

You'll also notice a better sense of well-being after you breathe from your diaphragm. It helps you in general and makes you feel great. It helps on many fronts and will benefit you greatly.

Using Diaphragmic Breathing with Meditation

Now, remember in the previous chapter when we said using diaphragmic breathing with meditation is possible? We'll discuss that there.

The best way to do it is either through breathing meditation where you sit down and focus on your breathing, or even, after a long day with many meetings, close your eyes, and from there, breathe in deeply for five seconds, and then breathe out for 10 seconds. Once you start breathing in, you might notice the heart rate increasing, and as you breathe out, from there it'll decrease. This helps to naturally stabilize the body, and increase both intention and attention as well.

Doing this on its own, or even just with your body in different places, such as in the shower, or even when walking around can prove to be incredibly beneficial.

I like to do this sometimes in the shower. I'll close my eyes, and become mindful of the body as I breathe in deeply, and from there, breathe out as well. I become mindful of the world around me, and my breathing, which in turn will change the way I handle various aspects of life. Diaphragmic breathing helps with handling all of the different changes, and aspects of life.

One great way to utilize this type of breathing is with a guided meditation. Sometimes, turning on a guided meditation before you begin will help you focus. I've done this before, and it helps immensely with keeping me grounded and focused. It also promotes the right mindset when doing this.

Sometimes, guided meditations also include breathing too, and you can do diaphragmic breathing while following along with this.

Sometimes, when you've got a few moments of downtime, diaphragmic breathing can be used. I like to do it sometimes when I'm in the car on the way home from work and I'm stuck in traffic. Just make sure you're paying attention to the road as you do it.

I also think using diaphragmic breathing with other meditations is incredibly beneficial. For example, I like to do this with loving-kindness meditation. That's because, as I'm experiencing the love flowing in, I can breathe in deeply, and from there as I send my love out to others, I can from there breathe out in a deep, and controlled manner.

No matter how you do this, no matter what type of breathing you do, breathing from your diaphragm will change things. Instead of breathing from your chest, breathe with a deeper focus on the way your diaphragm moves, and how it goes up and then goes down.

You'll feel the difference right away. You can do this during downtime as well. If you have a few minutes to relax, you can do this, and it can markedly help too.

For Those Who are Busy a Lot

I get it, a lot of us may not have much downtime to do this. But that's where breaks come in. during your breaks at work, you can use diaphragmic breathing in order to ground yourself. If you don't have the time or the drive to do meditations, you can use this. To do it, you can sit down in your chair, close your eyes, and from there, just breathe from your diaphragm for about 5-10 minutes at a time. Sometimes, having some music that plays in the background helps too with calming down, especially if you live a life where you're constantly moving from one point to another.

I also think after that, take a moment to not do something super mentally stimulating, such as listen to a song. This way, you're turning off the sympathetic nervous system for a moment or so, and from there, letting the parasympathetic nervous system, and the vagus nerve, work together in order to help relax and stimulate the body in a relaxed manner.

Sometimes, after a long meeting doing this will help ground you. It’s also great to do after a long day of work, before your drive home. Even just doing this right before you go to bed is a wonderful way to help stimulate your vagus nerve, promote sleep, and reduce inflammation.

If you have trouble implementing this, try to incorporate a schedule into this. Schedules are a great way to improve your wellness and happiness's and to stimulate the vagus nerve. I know a lot of people struggle with schedules, but they can prove to be quite wonderful, and are helpful for even the busiest people. Scheduling out just five minutes of diaphragmic breathing is wonderful, helpful for people, and can improve your mental state too. You don’t have to sit around and do an hour of meditation. Though, it might help you in some cases.

When looking to stimulate your vagus nerve in simple ways, this is one of the best ways to do it. It’ll clear the mind, and if you combine with meditation, you'll see the difference right away. Most don't realize the power this has, but as you work with this, you'll feel the difference right away, and from there stimulate your vagus nerve properly, and better than ever before. If nothing else, it'll help with meditation, and make it possible for you to open up the neural pathways, and activate your parasympathetic nervous system.

CHAPTER 11. INFLAMMATION AND VAGUS NERVE

Inflammation is something that happens within the body when there is a response to something that shouldn't be there.

Is all Inflammation Bad?

Not necessarily. In fact, inflammation is very important for making sure you respond to different stimuli within the body correctly.

With inflammation, you have either an injury, or a pain, or even an infection, and from this, you get more white blood cells, immune cells, and cytokines that are used for infection.

Inflammation is something that should be short-term, with redness, heat, swelling, and pain. But, in some cases, you might have inflammation happening within the body, without symptoms you normally don't notice.

When there is something in the body the brain recognizes as an invader, it starts the inflammation in the body. However, when not properly turned off, it can cause a lot of problems.

What conditions does it Cause?

Well, anything that yields an inflammatory response is a culprit here. For example, diabetes, heart disease, cancer, fatty liver disease, asthma, Chron's disease, IBS, and pretty much anything with inflammation as the cause is a part of this.

Food allergies and sensitivities are also seen here. Insulin resistance is another symptom of inflammation, hence why type 1 diabetes is often a result of inflammation in the body.

While some of the inflammation can be turned off quite easily, you'll realize that, with every single stimulus, it can actually make a lot of issues for people, and it can have a lot of problems that are very hard to fix if you're not careful.

People who are obese, or under a lot of stress, usually there is chronic inflammation there.

While you might notice it, most of the time you have to see a doctor to get some blood tests, including the C-reactive protein test, TMF alpha, and the IL-6, all of which are different chemicals that are within the body whenever you have an inflammatory response.

So, What Causes It?

Well, there are many different causes here, and the vagus nerve is actually a part of this. When the vagus nerve is properly stimulated, it sends out the neurotransmitters to tell the inflammatory response that it's over, the invader is gone, you don't need to activate, which causes a reduced response.

But, with a vagus nerve that's improperly stimulated, it can cause you to have overstimulation of the inflammatory response within the body, resulting in insulin resistance, heart disease, obesity, and also other conditions.

This is partially caused by your diet of course. Eating high amounts of sugars, carbs, high fructose corn syrup, and consuming a diet that's riddled with junk food is a part of the reason why you might have inflammatory responses, and the solution, in that case, is, of course, a diet change.

If you're stressed, and continuously activating the parasympathetic nervous system, your vagus nerve will be affected too. This, in turn, causes an inflammatory response in the body too, and hence, diseases will come forth too.

But, it's more than just the sugars. It's also how your vagus nerve is stimulated. When your vagus nerve isn't working, it won't control the inflammatory response, and oftentimes won't control the signals to the brain. This will, in turn, lead to debilitating conditions in the boy as we've discussed before.

In many instances, when we're continually reducing our "flight or fight" responses, the biological markers will help with reducing inflammation.

When you see a doctor for inflammation, chances are they won't prescribe medications for that. That's because the way to combat inflammation can't always be handled with medication, and oftentimes, medications cause more side effects than help to the body.

The vagus nerve affects your heart rate, and also acetylcholine, which is a tranquilizer that you can administer to yourself simply through inhaling and exhaling, and from there, your parasympathetic nervous system will be activated.

When you activate this, you're essentially encouraging the "rest and digest" or the "tend and befriend" actions in the body. The "tend and befriend" actions within your body, of course, are those neurotransmitters that are activated.

When you activate your vagus nerve, you're basically turning off all of those responses you don't need in the body, and it'll help with inflammation.

CHAPTER 12. VAGUS NERVE AND EMOTIONS

Vagus Nerve and empathy

Loving and kindness is all about creating compassion. The term "loving-kindness" is translated from the Pali word "Metta." Metta itself has numerous interpretations in Pali and they are benevolence, friendliness, friendship, good will, kindness, and love. The word Metta itself is a shortened form of "metta bhavana," meaning "developing loving-kindness." But what does Pali have to do with anything? Well, Pali is the language used by the Buddhists to record their scriptures, traditions, and beliefs.

When the loving-kindness meditation was first introduced, it was a way of self-healing, sweetening, and soothing the mind, and it helped produce positive feelings towards one's surroundings. It provides the power to eliminate negativity and go about our days with a positive aura. Did someone cut you off in your lane? Whatever. Your order arrived late? Why, you didn't even notice! Did your boss say something nasty to you in the office? Well, that is his opinion, and you know you are better than that.

The loving-kindness meditation isn’t just about your perspective on life. It is how you look at yourself and the way you treat yourself. For example, have you been overly critical of yourself recently? Perhaps you might have thought that using such an approach might motivate you into doing better or maybe you felt that you were constantly not achieving your goals. When you are critical, you are not achieving anything except teaching your mind negative attributes about yourself. You are viewing yourself under a poor light and this eventually will become your mindset about yourself. Once you form that negative mindset, it becomes difficult to revert back to a positive mindset. And negativity has an effect on your body as well. Primarily, it leads to the buildup of stress and anxiety.

Advantages of Loving-Kindness

Less self-criticism and self-destructive thoughts

You do not give yourself any opportunity for self-harm and self-criticism as soon as you commit to this meditation. You quieten your inner critic and make yourself a person willing to accept yourself even more.

Over time, when you invest time in loving-kindness meditation, you will be less affected by harmful thoughts, including those about causing harm to yourself or worse, taking your own life. You are going to view yourself in a different light and accept yourself wholly. Here is the simple truth: your life is precious, even if your thoughts seem to convince you otherwise. Going and seeking professional help is not a sign of weakness, but rather a sign of acceptance and of your willingness to be stronger and better. Additionally, along with professional help, not only do you take care of yourself better, but the combination of professional treatment and loving-kindness meditation is like getting Captain America and Iron Man together; it's a powerful combination.

More resilience

Having mental strength means that you can deal with numerous mental challenges with better capabilities. For example, do you feel the effects of stress? Instead of feeling like you won't be able to do anything about it, you become a person of action, thinking of ways to combat it or deal with it. Anxiety attacks don't send you into a state of frenzy. You become a master of learning how to calm your anxious thoughts.

Practicing Compassion Meditation

- Find a comfortable position in which you can sit for the duration of the meditation. You can also choose to lie down, but people have often found that they end up drifting off to sleep from the meditation.

- As you allow your eyes to gently close, focus on your body and make any minor adjustments. If you find yourself uncomfortable sitting on the floor, then you can use a chair as well.
- We are going to begin with a few minutes of concentration practice, just to help our minds calm down and arrive in our present time. If you remember our earlier meditation technique, then use that right here in order to calm your mind. Don't be in a hurry and allow your thoughts to settle down. You don't have to meditate for 15-20 minutes. You just need 5 minutes of meditation to get your mind to discard any negativity or distracting thoughts. Once you have succeeded in doing that, it is time to get to the

next step in the meditation process.

- Bring your mind to yourself as you sit here right now. Try to connect with your own deepest intentions for happiness, calmness, and safety. Connect with that natural desire of happiness that you would like to see. If you like, you can even think back to certain happy thoughts. These could be something that happened to you in your past or even something that you had done. For example, let us say that you showed some charity towards a person begging on the street. Any moment that you felt good about or brought some joy into your life can be helpful in this moment. But the trick is to not dwell on the memory, but the feelings that those memories bring to you.

- Focus on those feelings as you breathe steadily. Make sure that you are not breathing too fast or your brain might interpret it as though you are nervous about something. Calm and steady breathing convinces your mind that there is nothing for it to be worried about.
- You can let this person go from your mind and bring to mind a neutral person. This is someone you see, maybe even regularly, but don't know very well. It may be somebody who works somewhere you go a lot, a coworker, or maybe a neighbor.
- Although you don't know this person well, you can recognize that this person wants to be happy as well. You don't need to know what their happiness looks like. Their happiness is their own. Regardless, you would like for

them to find that source of happiness. Again, offer this person the phrases of loving-kindness, connecting with the intention to care about their wellbeing.

Vagus nerve and socialization

Our quality of life is determined to a large extent by the quality of our social relationships and our ability to connect emotionally with others. Good relationships are great for your immunity in terms of fighting off diseases and infections and are also vital for your psychological and emotional health.

Establishing great social networks and sound relationships with your family and friends will significantly decrease depressive tendencies and improve your overall ability to cope with stress which as we have seen is a big factor in physical and mental disorders.

Research has proven that people with better relationships are happier, healthier and live longer. Your ventral vagus nerve, which is our social engagement or "smart" nerve improves our ability to connect with others emotionally and enables us to develop socially acceptable behavior and emotional reactions.

Having good relationships will not only help you deal with stress effectively, but it will also decrease stress-related conditions such as chronic inflammation, depression, and social anxiety. Research has shown that lonely people are more prone to depression and have a lower body immunity which makes them more prone to infections and diseases.

Work on building good relationships, connecting emotionally with people and being socially open. It will go a long in improving your mental health, emotional outlook, and physical wellbeing.

Vagus nerve and anxiety

When the vagus nerve is stimulated it causes a response which reduces stress. Vagus nerve stimulation helps to reduce the heart rate as well as blood pressure.

It also stimulates functioning in different parts of the brain as well as digestion which helps us to feel more relaxed. This is all known as the vagal response.

Simply put the vagal response is simply what happens when the vagus nerve is stimulated. When the nerve is stimulated it helps to reduce anxiety. Amazingly yoga masters were using these techniques long before scientists even knew about the vagal response.

Researchers have found that by stimulating the vagus nerve regularly anxiety, as well as stress, can be reduced. On top of this, it can also help reduce the symptoms or even neutralize COPD, asthma, and heart disease.

This should provide us with some comfort at least. These researchers are quickly learning that not only is our physical health completely in our control, but our mental health is as well. Studies have shown that people who suffer from mental disorders as well as chronic illnesses such as COPD, benefit from Vagus Nerve stimulation.

There is actual science to back up the vagal response. We talked previously about the fight or flight response and how it can put a person on edge. This is the same response that you feel when a person cuts you off while you are driving or when the cashier can't seem to ring up your order right no matter how many times she tries.

This response has helped to keep humans alive over the years but as we learned it can also cause a lot of damage when it is experienced too often. It is then when we do not feel that we are ever really able to relax that we need to start stimulating the Vagus Nerve.

While stimulating the vagus nerve may sound like it is going to be very complicated the truth is that it really is not that hard. The good news is that it also gets easier the more that you do it.

Vagus nerve and stress level

Imagine that you're at work, plugging away and completing what you're supposed to. Suddenly your boss sends you a message requesting that you complete these other items by the end of the day. You can handle it, so you take on those additional tasks. Within the next few minutes, you realize that they're a whole lot larger than you thought they were going to be, so you start to feel overwhelmed. Maybe an hour later, your child's school calls, saying that little Kate is sick and needs to go home. Suddenly you have a full plate with work and a sick child to care for, and your original feeling of being overwhelmed is now a full-blown feeling of being stressed.

Your body starts to release all these hormones that increase your feelings of stress. Your blood pressure rises, your heart rate increases, and your muscles get tense. This is your sympathetic nervous system coming online to help you deal with the dangerous situation. However, there isn't any actual danger, just a lot of work. Your brain, though, sees this situation as dangerous and puts you in the beginning stages of fight or flight, causing your ventral vagus nerve to retreat.

Eventually, once your work is completed and little Kate is better, your brain will tell your ventral vagus that the threat has passed, and your vagus nerve will hit the brakes on your stress response, giving you feelings of calm and well-being, while reducing your heart rate and breathing rate.

This feeling is probably familiar to you. You may not even be aware of the changes in your physiology until you've been stressed for a while. By that point, you've been operating in a high alert state for a bit and then need your vagus nerve to step in. But if your brain still thinks there's a threat, then it won't. The fact is that your body will reactivate its sympathetic nervous system again and again anytime it perceives a threat, including just feeling overwhelmed at work. This frequent activation of being always on alert can do damage to your body. Your heart can start to feel strain, your hormones can cause your blood pressure to remain high, and you are at more risk for cardiovascular issues and obesity. If you experience high amounts of stress every day, then this is how your body responds to it.

Vagus nerve and epilepsy

In 1997, the FDA permitted the utilization of vagus nerve incitement for hard-headed epilepsy.

This includes a little, electrical gadget, like a pacemaker, being put in an individual's chest. A slight wire known as a lead keeps running from the gadget to the vagus nerve.

The gadget is put in the body by medical procedure under general soporific. It at that point sends electrical driving forces at customary interims, for the duration of the day, to the mind by means of the vagus nerve to decrease the seriousness, or even stop, seizures.

Vagus nerve incitement for epilepsy may have some symptoms including sore throat and trouble gulping.

Symptoms of vagus nerve incitement for epilepsy include:

- hoarseness or changes in voice
- sore throat
- shortness of breath
- coughing
- slow pulse
- difficulty gulping
- stomach uneasiness or queasiness

Individuals utilizing this type of treatment ought to consistently tell their primary care physician and when they are having any issues as there might be approaches to lessen or stop these.

Quantum Brain Healing depends on a base of orthomolecular medication including amino acids, nutrients, minerals, herbs, plant removes, Chinese natural recipes, and numerous elective treatments. There is no answer that will address recuperating for everybody. It is constantly key to stay open to innovation when different alternatives have not met our objectives. One alternative that can be cared for attempting dietary treatment is Vagus Nerve Stimulation. This is a therapeutic gadget that is carefully embedded. Any significant restorative focus in the US and Europe can embed this gadget for a patient that qualifies.

Vagus Nerve Stimulation (VNS) includes making an impression on the cerebrum utilizing occasional gentle electrical incitement from the vagus nerve in the neck by a precisely embedded little restorative gadget. There is no mind medical procedure included. This incitement or heartbeat is sent by a therapeutic gadget like a pacemaker. The vagus nerve is a piece of the autonomic sensory system and controls automatic body capacities.

VNS may control epilepsy in situations where against epileptic medications are insufficient or have unbearable reactions, or neurosurgery isn't suitable for reasons unknown. VNS is viable in halting seizures in certain patients.

The embedded restorative gadget is a level, round battery, and measures about the size of a silver dollar. The VNS therapeutic gadget was created by Cyberonics, Inc. The specialist decides the quality and timing of the beats controlled by the gadget as indicated by every patient's individual needs. The degree of electrical incitement can be changed without extra medical procedure with a programming wand associated with a Workstation.

The symptoms of VNS during treatment may incorporate raspiness, hacking, throat torment, brevity of breath, a short and slight impression of gagging, changed voice sound, ear torment, tooth torment, and a shivering sensation in the neck. Skin disturbance or disease could happen at the implantation site. VNS doesn't contrarily affect the mind. This is significant medical procedure and ought not be considered gently. For those with wild epileptic seizures, it might be last alternative. Think about all choices before abandoning controlling seizure.

CONCLUSION

Sometimes, and maybe more often than we care to admit to ourselves, the easily accessible power that the vagus nerve holds to reduce inflammation and anxiety gets underestimated and overlooked as a method of balanced treatment for the body.

We are often far too quick to reach for Ibuprofen and Prozac, and don't always realize that we have to tools to balance our lives right in the palm of...well, not our hands specifically, but in our nervous system and waiting to be used.

You could almost go as far as to say that the vagus nerve has its own type of 'yin yang' factor to it.

By this I mean that with the vagus nerve we have both the sympathetic and parasympathetic nervous systems that are opposites in what they do. On the sympathetic side, you have you fight or flight mode that gives you a burst of adrenaline and cortisol in order to pounce on whatever may be about to attack you (currently in my case, a spider that is eyeballing me from the wall opposite where I am sitting), while on the other hand, your parasympathetic nerve which allows you to relax and lower your breathing and heart rate after the burst of energy previously felt. (I think I will name him Michael). So when Michael decides to shimmey his way back out the window to his little spider family, my parasympathetic nervous system can kick in and allow me to breathe again!

The tug of war in a push and pull fight between these two sides of the nervous system thus creates the ultimate balance within your body with homeostasis.

If we go back in time, and I mean many, many years, we could look at the possibilities from an evolutionary perspective, too. We could probably say that our ancestors relied on the sympathetic nervous system in order to get their instincts for hunting as well as to stay safe against any enemies that could potentially attack them or steal their food supply.

On the other hand, the parasympathetic nervous system probably allowed others in the family tree to bond between and make sure that the family was cared for as well as to ensure procreation of the next generation and build supportive communities amongst themselves.

Sadly, for the rest of us, the 21st century has caused a lot of change over a short period of time that we, as the next generation, have had to struggle to keep up with the times.

This in turn is causing our systems to completely short circuit more often than not, and we are having to go all out to keep the balance necessary for our body's survival. Our nervous systems have no idea what is going on these days! Recent studies have shown that social media and other modern-day technological factors are causing far more social isolation, anxiety, depression, and feelings of being unworthy of love. On top of that, we have made it a habit to have “every man for himself” becoming the norm which can also throw off some people’s fight and flight responses, as you don’t have anyone that you can turn to should you need physical or emotional help.

Fortunately, the last few generations have figured out how we can use the vagus nerve to our benefit, and this is slowly developing its way into a full rolling therapy treatment for many people. Researchers are still to this day and minute finding new ways to use the vagus nerve to our advantage, and tweaking it in just the right way to get the full power.

What is marvelous about this life balancing technique of vagus nerve stimulation is that it doesn’t have to cost you a cent. With most cases being something that you can stimulate your nerve with at home and only a few that require a vagus nerve stimulator, it can put the power into your own hands and allow for a better quality of life overall.

CPSIA information can be obtained
at www.ICGtesting.com
Printed in the USA
LVHW050341210423
744868LV00002B/121

9 781806 312405